RECIPE OF MEMORY

RECIPE *of* MEMORY

five generations of

MEXICAN CUISINE

Victor M. Valle and Mary Lau Valle

Foreword by Elena Poniatowska

THE NEW PRESS NEW YORK

LIBRARY OF CONGRESS CATALOGING-IN-PUBLICATION DATA

 Valle, Victor M.
  Recipe of memory: five generations of Mexican cuisine /
   Victor M. Valle and Mary Lau Valle.
   p.   cm.
 ISBN 1-56584-126-3
  1. Cookery, Mexican. 2. Cookery, Mexican—History—19th century.
  3. Guadalajara (Mexico)—Social life and customs.
  I. Valle, Mary Lau. II. Title.
 TX716.M4V35
 641.5972—dc2095-10825
 CIP

PUBLISHED IN THE UNITED STATES BY THE NEW PRESS, NEW YORK
DISTRIBUTED BY W. W. NORTON & COMPANY, INC., NEW YORK

Established in 1990 as a major alternative to the large, commercial publishing houses,
The New Press is the first full-scale nonprofit
American book publisher outside of the university presses.

The Press is operated editorially in the public interest,
rather than for private gain; it is committed to publishing
in innovative ways works of educational,
cultural, and community value that, despite their intellectual merits,
might not normally be commercially viable.

The New Press's editorial offices are located
at the City University of New York.

book design, HALL SMYTH; illustrations, GORDON WHITESIDE
production management, KIM WAYMER

printed in the UNITED STATES of AMERICA

95 96 97 98 9 8 7 6 5 4 3 2 1

For Estela, who saved a history
of flavors in her cedar chest,
and a place at table for all of us;
And for Julio, second bridge
to a century of ghosts, and generous
innkeeper to wandering relations
who asked us this before dying:

Did they pass the Proposition,
did fear decree one more pogrom?
His children and grandchildren
held his hand and promised no.
And they will keep their word—six
generations of love will not be broken,
a continent of memory cannot be divided.

COMIDA

uno se come
la luna en la tortilla
comes fríjol
y comes tierra
comes chile
y comes sol y fuego
bebes agua
y bebes cielo

one eats
the moon in a tortilla
eat frijoles
and you eat earth
eat chile
and you eat sun and fire
drink water
and you drink sky

FOOD

—Victor Valle

CONTENTS

Foreword: Gastronomy as History

TODAY MORE THAN EVER, the art of cooking has acquired the same status as that of history itself. Behind every recipe lies the Battle of Waterloo, the Civil War, the Mexican Revolution, the entire history of a family, the family tree of a dynasty. At least this is the case with Victor and Mary Valle's delightful book *Recipe of Memory.*

In the pages you are about to read, every recipe is carefully situated within its appropriate historical and domestic context. We learn not only how to prepare the delicious entrees but also a bit of the history of the Mexican provinces in which they were created, along with the particular—and for the non-Mexican reader, perhaps peculiar—customs and traditions that accompany and adorn its delectation. Such is the case for the recipe for Drunk Chickens from Aguascalientes, where the bird is slowly cooked in *pulque*, thus creating a gastronomic delight out of an entree that many are accustomed only to eating roasted, fried, or grilled.

The state of Jalisco and its august capital city, Guadalajara, are probably the two most creative sites of Mexican culture and gastronomy. Two universal geniuses were born in Jalisco: the painter José Clemente Orozco, famous for his heart-wrenching murals depicting the plight of the Mexican underclass, and the writer Juan Rulfo, who immortalized the region through his novel *Pedro Páramo,* arguably the most important literary work of modern Mexican fiction. The novelists Agustín Yañez and Olivia Zuniga are also from Jalisco, as well as the jeweler-turned-storyteller Juan José Arreola, the literary critic Emmanuel Carballo, and the essayist José Luis Martínez. All five gave themselves to the carnal pleasures of the table. In his home town of Guadalajara, the magician of crepe paper, José (Chucho) Reyes Ferreira, opened an antique shop before dedicating himself to the art of painting. His flowers and angels were like meringues and whipped cream. Juan Soriano, the gourmet who for years was considered the *enfant terrible* of Mexican bohemia and a painter loved by all, also was born in Guadalajara. Lupe Marín, possibly the most fascinating woman of all Mexico, wife of Diego Rivera, the panther with emerald eyes who seduced the Spanish writer and intellectual Ramón del Valle Inclan when he came from Spain to Mexico, was also from Jalisco, and was an extraordinary artist in the kitchen. Mexicans still remember her chiles stuffed with cheese.

Is it a coincidence that so many artistic and literary figures emerged out of Jalisco and Guadalajara or was there something magically nourishing about the food of the region? Jalisco, like the cloud-filled skies captured by the camera of Gabriel Figueroa, is enchanting and imponderable. Much of its unique character surely is owed to what its inhabitants eat: the famous barbecued lamb dish known as *birria*; *posole*, a hearty soup made with pork, chicken, and huge kernels of corn; royal meat balls; not to mention the pickled pigeons. A slight variation on a popular Mexican saying might be: "Tell me what you eat and I'll tell you who you are." The inhabitants of Jalisco eat to the rhythmic sounds of mariachis who sing from the beginning to the end of the meal, from the first soup to the last dessert. Even though the saying goes "He who sings and dines, when he gets up loses his mind," music and song accompany each succulent mouthful and soothe its digestion, sweetening and calming the humors.

Not only do Victor and Mary Valle give us the recipe, which in itself is a most generous gift (many Mexican families keep recipes handed down for generations a top secret), they also tell us about the house in which these dishes are eaten, the color of the patio's adobe walls, and bougainvilleas, calla lilies, geraniums that thrive in the hallway planters. Their grandparents and great-grandparents would feel very content because here, next to the *sapote* flavored ice cream, the sweet milk made from *camote* (sweet potato) and almond, are the stories of a past, of a Mexico that, for better or worse, we have not yet been able to surpass.

Elena Poniatowska
Chimalistac, Mexico D.F., June 1995

ACKNOWLEDGMENTS

This book could not have been written without the guidance and unswerving faith of the following people: My mother, Lilly, for being my grandmother's best cooking student, and for acknowledging my intuitions even when it hurt; and my father for having the courage to always speak the truth. We express our unending love to our daughters, Lucena and Alexandra, for their patience, curiosity, and, above all, their worldly palates. We could always rely on you to point out our successes and our failures. May you enjoy the book and add to it in your later years. And to Tomás and Josefina Lau, know that you still teach us much about possibilities, paradoxes, and countless antidotes to culinary boredom. You possessed the wisdom and good taste to invent a new *mestizo* cuisine from two of the world's oldest, the Chinese and Mexican.

Our boundless gratitude to Dawn Davis for her tireless efforts to create a new literature. We would also like to thank Dan Strehl and colleagues at the Los Angeles Public Library. The Latino, community of Los Angeles owes you a great debt for believing that its residents deserved the nation's most extensive collection of Mexican, Latino, and Hispanic culinary literature. And finally, thanks to Christopher Caldwell for helping us find a publisher, Richard Kahlenberg for believing in your vision of California literature, Rudy Torres for your scholarly counsel, Margarita Nieto for listening so patiently, and George Sánchez and a new generation of Latino social historians, without whose help this book could not have been written.

FAMILY TREE

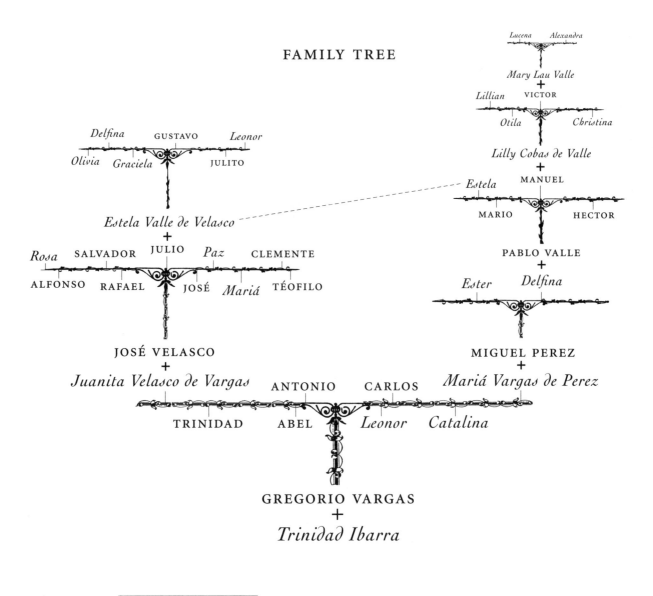

Lucena   *Alexandra*

Mary Lau Valle
+
Lillian   VICTOR
Otila   *Christina*

Lilly Cobas de Valle
+
Estela   MANUEL
MARIO   HECTOR

PABLO VALLE
+
Ester   *Delfina*

MIGUEL PEREZ
+
Mariá Vargas de Perez

Delfina   GUSTAVO   *Leonor*
Olivia   *Graciela*   JULITO

Estela Valle de Velasco
+
Rosa   SALVADOR   JULIO   *Paz*   CLEMENTE
ALFONSO   RAFAEL   JOSÉ   *Mariá*   TÉOFILO

JOSÉ VELASCO
+
Juanita Velasco de Vargas

ANTONIO   CARLOS
TRINIDAD   ABEL   *Leonor*   *Catalina*

GREGORIO VARGAS
+
Trinidad Ibarra

| *Female* | 〜〜〜 | + |
| MALE | Siblings | Marriage |

ASCENT LINES ILLUSTRATE ONLY THOSE FAMILY
MEMBERS DIRECTLY RELATED TO BOOK'S NARRATIVE.

MEXICO AND THE SOUTHWESTERN UNITED STATES, CIRCA 1850

PART ONE

Guadalajara

I suppose pleasures of the table can be called 'carnal' pleasures,
and the Chinese people with their own
down-to-earth philosophy have always regarded eating
as one of the things which reconcile us to this earthly life.
It is this philosophy which enables the Chinese
to discuss pork and philosophy under the same rubric
and praise a man's philosophy but condemn his fillet.
It takes a Latin temperament to appreciate this.

LIN YUTANG

a family of recipes

THE FEAST BEGAN WITH a blur of wings. Days before, my grandmother Delfina had decided to rid herself of the pigeons crowding the old coop that leaned precariously against my aunt's backyard fence. I must have been at least eight years old when I looked up into the tall coop and the feather-tufted plywood boxes. Inside them squirmed plump young birds, which to me looked like wrinkled old men.

Delfina lived in her daughter's house in Canta Ranas (Singing Frogs), a Southeast Los Angeles barrio of Mexican families that occupied the lower ground on the east bank of the San Gabriel River. Before the oil boom of 1920, before the flood control projects of the early 1950s, Canta Ranas had sprung up along the river as a makeshift labor camp for Mexican citrus workers. Later, modest wood frame houses replaced the flimsy workers' shanties on the flood plain once over-run by the San Gabriel, by legions of toads and frogs. Hence the barrio's name, one worthy of a Maya village where croaking frogs announce a downpour.

But my grandmother had other animals in mind when she called on her sons and nephews to slaughter the innocents that now overcrowded their coop. She was busy setting a feast in motion. I missed the killing, but not the acrid smell of wet feathers and bloodied water. Nor the chores to which my cousin and I were assigned—clearing out the abandoned grocery store where the meal would be served. A confusion of smells—overripe fruit, stale *cilantro*, moldy onion—lingered there with the dust that began to circulate upward as my cousin and I made our way through the room's clutter of old furniture and splintered saw horses. No merchandise remained. Only the basket for catching items once stocked in the shelves hung from pulleys, lodged against a long pole with insectlike mandibles. My grandmother used to lock the pole's rusted pincers upon merchandise she brought down from dusty shelves. Next door, in the shade of my Aunt Estela's patio, my father and his brothers had their hands full—literally—of gray down as they plucked and dressed dozens of birds.

Afterward, my grandmother simmered the squabs with parsley, onion, and garlic in her large, weathered pot. She cooked the rice in the broth of the squabs, adding freshly ground cloves, cinnamon, and saffron. Finally, minutes before serving, she returned the squabs to simmer again in the broth and rice suffused with the paella-like spices. The trick, my aunt recalls, was leaving enough broth to flavor the squab without drying out the rice.

In the meantime, my cousin and I had cleared enough space in the empty store for some benches and a long row of tables. By early evening, when everyone else had arrived, my grandmother and aunt proudly made their entrance with platters of quartered squab on a bed of fire-orange rice. Garnishes of raw, sliced onion immersed in vinegar, salt, and a hint of oregano, and gallon jars of iced and sweetly sour *jamaica* (hibiscus tea) also appeared at the table. My grandmother took her customary pleasure in serving my uncles, cousins, aunts, and my eldest sister, who wasn't quite sold on the idea of eating baby birds. Midway through the meal, Estela says, Delfina made everyone laugh by recounting how her first try at getting rid of the pigeons had failed. The birds had returned to their old coop, flying all the way back from her brother-in-law's house a dozen or so miles away in Artesia.

I'm not sure what else Delfina prepared. My Aunt Estela, Delfina's daughter, says the meal would have opened with steamy bowls of *puchero*, a hearty soup swimming with carrots, turnips, zucchini, parsley, beef bones, some chicken, and garbanzo or rice, which Delfina cooked in the pot tea-bag-style, by placing the grains in small cheesecloth sacks. A simple lettuce salad dressed with olive oil and vinegar might have preceded the main course. The whole affair would have certainly ended with a *sancocho de guayaba*, a homey dessert of halved Mexican guavas stewed in cinnamon and *piloncillo*, an unrefined, flavorful sugar.

But it was the taste of squab and saffron that stayed with me longest. I found the faintly bitter, smoky intensity of saffron, made bolder with cinnamon and clove, intoxicating. Between bites of pickled onion I sucked off dark meat from diminutive bones, and probably stained my shirt. Afterward, the tables were pushed aside and our parents began to dance. I laid my head on Delfina's broad lap and fell asleep as she smoothed my forehead, preparing me for the dreaming.

For the day of the feast, Delfina had turned to the recipes of Catalina Clementina Vargas, her aunt, the woman who had taken charge of her education years ago in Guadalajara. She had unearthed one *Sopa de pichones* (squab on saffron rice), a recipe Catalina had recorded in a book with 108 others in an elegant elliptical script, which she dated June 7, 1888. Catalina's cookbook wasn't the only one in Delfina's possession. A year before she married in 1908, Delfina and a cousin copied another 141 recipes from a cookbook collected by Catalina's mother, Trinidad.

As time went on, and Delfina married, raised her own family, and migrated to Los Angeles, she collected her own recipes, adding to Catalina and Trinidad's legacy.

Together, these three women had passed along a family of more than 250 recipes that offer a revealing glimpse of Guadalajara's culinary history. Of the three, Catalina's recipes show the strongest connection to the Mexican cookbooks published during the nineteenth century. Trinidad's recipes, by contrast, reveal the region's provincial cuisine. Hers was the kind of satisfying day-to-day cooking served to family, or prepared in advance for the family outings to nearby Lake Chapala or a stay with relatives at their hacienda in nearby Zapotlanejo, or for the guests at her husband's inn.

The recipes collected by Delfina reflect a double transition—revolution and migration. On the one hand, her recipes show new indigenous culinary influences that rushed into Guadalajara during and after the revolution of 1910 with the arrival of thousands of newcomers from surrounding Indian and *mestizo* towns. On the other hand, the recipes reflect the culinary ideas, like pancakes, she adopted upon crossing the United States border.

How all of these recipes crossed the border, and what these recipes say about the women who wrote them, intrigued and inspired my wife and I to untangle the relationships among Catalina, Trinidad, Delfina, and their descendants. Untangling this web of stories and recipes passed on to me by my Aunt Estela gave form to *Recipe of Memory*.

Not surprisingly, this book mimics Mexican cuisine, blending the genres of personal memoir and social history with a family cookbook. It also mixes narratives, sometimes pursuing the logic of linear chronology, at other moments

PAGE FROM CATALINA'S COOKBOOK.

following memory's elusive threads and sudden apparitions. And it mixes voices — my own, which tells the story of a family of recipe writers — and those of my wife, Mary, who expertly researched, interpreted, and translated these recipes for English-speaking readers.

IN MANY WAYS, CATALINA'S AND TRINIDAD'S recipes reflect a particular moment in Western Mexico's culinary history. In the late nineteenth century, Guadalajara's cuisine flourished when industrialization linked it to new foreign fashions, products, and markets. Thus, however much some of its "educated" citizens bemoaned their city's lack of well-ordered European uniformity, Guadalajara's cuisine thrived expressly because of its jarring and sometimes dazzling *inclusions*.

By the late 1880s, the century's industrial bounty was displayed in the shop windows, lighted by electricity: plumed bonnets, shampoo, tall black toppers, safety matches, canned baby peas, champagne, circular pointed pens, daguerreotypes, stereoscopic slides, *cartes de visite*, whalebone corsets, butterfly ties, full-length crinoline gowns, long English drawing jackets, and short French dress coats, much of this now brought by steamships and steam engines.

IN THE SPIRIT OF THIS DECADE OF CHANGE, an emergent middle class pursued education as a means to clothe themselves in a new social respectability and produced a generation of illustrious intellectuals and artists who later would educate a generation of revolutionaries.

Many of Guadalajara's wealthy families, by contrast, didn't fret over social validation. Like the walled-in patios of their old homes, they isolated themselves in ignorant arrogance. The culinary appetites of this once landed gentry preferred their own version of home cooking: the wholesome simplicity of ancestral Spanish recipes such as the *fiambres*, or the cold meat dishes, the paella-like rice dishes such as *Sopa de pichones*, and *puchero*, a distinctly Spanish version of vegetable-beef soup.

However, more progressive members of the city's social elite formed new business partnerships with English, American, and Latin American capitalists, which they solidified with marriages. They promoted an openness to the new American and European ideas, including mock turtle soup and roast beef. Rather than wall themselves in, these families built smart, spacious homes in the best art nouveau designs on wide tree-shaded avenues on the outskirts of the city. They reproduced neoclassical elegance and art nouveau romanticism in the banquets they set before visiting dignitaries, presidents, and industrial tycoons. Europe's new image was bourgeois, industrial, and Victorian. Good taste meant sober, mathematical symmetry—even in food.

Outside their homes, the city's streets and plazas were permeated with the fragrances of guavas and *zapotes*, and the aroma of burnt chiles, roast corn, spicy sizzling sausages, or joints of pork boiling in caldrons filled with smoky fat. Though their Tlaxcalteca, Coca, Otomi, Tepehua, and Tarascan names had been erased by conquest, the flavors of their indigenous cooking were strained into the mud floor market stalls and the plaza's basalt slabs. Myriad versions of green tomato enchiladas called *entotomadas*, fragrant pineapple wine called *tepache*, a Tarascan catfish stew called *caldo michi*, and *birria*, the whole goats redolent with chiles and cinnamon, and ginger baked in bread ovens, suggested the persistence of urban indigenous cuisines predating the European settlers.

In culinary terms, at least, the late nineteenth century marked a high point of Guadalajara's cuisine. The costs were high. The lavish banquets of the rich and the elaborate recipes of the middle class were sustained by an impoverished countryside, legions of enslaved servants, and housewives confined to their kitchens.

Thus, Catalina's ability to write down her recipes in a schooled Spanish signaled a subtle but crucial change over the grinding domesticity that characterized the lives of so many of her countrywomen. She represented a small but growing female elite that would acquire formal educations and launch careers. The same woman who wrote down recipes also composed poems and educated scores of Mexican women, including her niece, Delfina. All of these achievements show the empowering effects of the written word. Literacy not only enhanced Catalina's ability to act upon her world, it made her an example of independence and scholarship to her male and female descendants five generations later.

But I have to admit that the broader consequences of Catalina's example were not clear to

CATALINA SITTING FOR A PHOTOGRAPH IN
DON OCTAVIANO DE LA MORA'S STUDIO ON HER
TWELFTH BIRTHDAY, CIRCA 1874.

17

me as I pored over the recipes and documents my Aunt Estela had set out for me on her kitchen table. Nor did I fully appreciate her cookbook as a cultural and historical artifact. Instead, my curiosity was personal. I devoured the banquet of memory Estela prepared because I expected to discover my own reflection. Perhaps the recipes could tell me something about who I was. Equally important, this family archive patiently assembled by Delfina obliged me to reconsider the way I remembered my grandmother.

As a child, I only saw my grandmother's reassuring presence clothed in wash-worn print dresses and cinnamon stockings that sagged below her knees; saw only the matriarch of soft brown eyes and gray hair fibered with thick black threads. I didn't know that she was born in 1897, or that she had already lived a lifetime by the time she arrived in Canta Ranas with her daughter's family. She had survived a revolution, the Depression, and the death of her philandering husband, whom she buried in Guadalajara in 1932, before she returned to Los Angeles with her four children for a second time.

She quickly discovered, as other immigrants have since, that the pride of being a resident of Guadalajara counted for little in the fields, the mines, the sweatshops, the slaughterhouses, and servants' quarters of her new country. Yet she had the presence of mind not to give in, as others would, to the *espanto*, or soul loss, induced by cultural assimilation. Delfina resisted it until she died on February 20, 1972, at the age of seventy-five. I know now that her ability to read and write in Spanish better equipped her to defend my memories.

Delfina understood that her new country would turn her grandchildren progressively mute if they did not hold onto their family history. That's why the conversations she presided over in her daughter's kitchen were charged with so much meaning. My grandmother was there to coax from uncles and aunts, sons and daughters, the remembered fragrance of distant mango, *zapote*, and *chirimoya* trees. Delfina's remembering went beyond words. She brought them to life by re-creating a lushly chaotic microcosm of Jalisco's subtropic highlands within the confines of her daughter's garden in southeast Los Angeles. The smuggling of herbs, hard-to-get chile and squash seeds, sapling *guayaba* trees, and even parrots stuffed into purses, were other memory fragments my grandmother and aunts distributed from one household to another after each visit to Tijuana.

I resented the way my elders defended their memories. I wanted to fit in, to become "American." I didn't want to be reminded that my first language was Spanish. At school I quickly realized that speaking Spanish could have humiliating consequences. The punishment for repeating the most innocuous Spanish phrase was a swat from my junior high vice principal. But my parents were ruthless. They enforced Delfina's decree that her grandchildren read and write Spanish with Saturday lessons, which I hated. I felt not only deprived of prime playtime, but singled out as a kind of freak when my friends came to the door. Most of the Chicano kids in my barrio endured school as a punishment.

Yet, as different as my family was, the food my mother placed upon our table never embarrassed me. In fact, I got a thrill out of seeing the expression on a friend's face when we happened to run into the kitchen and discover a platter of my mother's *sopes*, palm-sized maize tortillas with crunchy ridges for holding in a layer of refried beans, followed by *chorizo*, diced tomato, onion, shredded cabbage, and *cilantro*. My mother topped these mounds of *crudités* with a few spoonfuls of a fiery *de arbol* chile and a generous pinch of crumbled *cotija* or Parmesan cheese. She then placed a half-dozen radish rosettes and a few scallions marinaded in lemon juice on the platter to accent the cubed crimsons, whites, and green heaped on the *sopes*. Invariably, my astonished Chicano friend would ask me what the appetizers were called. My answer provoked another question: Was this Mexican food? I'd say of course, and try to steal a *sope* or two, or else ask my mom if she'd let my friend taste one. Mom usually said yes, and won an admirer for life. My mother, Lilly, later told me that Delfina had taught

her to make *sopes* when my parents ran a *tortillería* in Tijuana. But the recipe, she added, came from Jalisco, my grandmother's home state.

My sensory education continued on Sundays when we visited my grandmother after mass. Because we were expected, Delfina had prepared something special, like *Conejo en huerto* (Rabbit in the Garden). Delfina had borrowed this stew, fragrant with quince, plantain, Spanish olives, roasted tomato, raisins, and pickled cauliflower, from one of Catalina's recipes with substitutions for rare ingredients such as *tejocotes*, a pungent, applelike fruit from central Mexico.

Delfina understood that the meals she served and the recipes she taught my mother constituted a language unto itself. With these magic formulas she sharpened my senses; with these written words she created memories strong enough to last until I was ready to ask where they'd come from. I realized this late one night a few months after arriving at Northwestern University. I looked out our ninth-floor apartment window, the L-train's red lights trailing off into the humid dark, turning the pages of Catalina's cookbook, which Estela had lent me, until I happened upon the *Sopa de pichones* recipe. At that moment I felt the energy of two deliberate acts — Catalina's decision to record the recipe and the skill with which Delfina revived it — telegraphed to me in a flash of recognition. A wave of questions had been set in motion.

CHAPTER TWO

food, politics, and family
at the inn of san felipe

TRINIDAD IBARRA DE VARGAS WAS BORN in Guadalajara in 1848. She bore seven children, four of them daughters, and died at age seventy in 1918, the year my father was born. A ghostly glass plate positive of cobalt and silver fixes a telling image of Trinidad—the dutiful young wife posing next to her husband, Gregorio [see following page]. The plate shows my great-great-grandmother to be in her early twenties. She wears a simple cotton blouse with puffed sleeves and a shawl around her shoulders. Trinidad is attractive, corpulent, with fine features and a squarish, high forehead accentuated by the symmetry of long, ribboned braids. Her eyes appear to cower slightly in her husband's presence. Subtle gradations in the plate's atomized pigments suggest Trinidad's cinnamon skin. A birth certificate classifies Trinidad as a *mestiza*, or one born of Spanish *and* Indian parents. The term's appearance on this document shows how the state enforced the system of racial castes. Gregorio sits stiffly next to her in a dark jacket, a rumpled white cotton shirt, and a limply knotted bow tie. His pale forehead betrays prolonged hat use under a blazing sun. He is fifteen years Trinidad's senior. His gaze is sternly authoritarian. His manly disregard for his appearance fits his calling as an innkeeper skilled at handling both lodgers and mule teams.

Gregorio's own words add important detail to the family portrait. He begins his fourteen-year-long chronicle of "Notable Events" in 1859 with what had to have been one of the most difficult periods in his life. On August 1 of that year, Gregorio's father dies in the midst of a seemingly endless civil war. The following year, the liberal supporters of President Benito Juarez begin to encircle Guadalajara, convinced that this bastion of conservatism must fall before taking Mexico City, and establishing a constitutional republic once and for all. It was during this period that Gregorio's brother, Antonio, goes to war. It's impossible to know for sure which side Antonio joined. I suspect that he signed up with the

besieged conservatives as a way of expressing his loyalty
to his city and his employer, Don José Palomar, a former conservative governor and wealthy industrialist who
owned the Inn of San Felipe. But gossip of mounting
conservative defeats may have inspired Antonio to escape
under the cover of night to join the liberal forces
encamped on the city's outskirts.

Like inns during the American revolutionary war,
their Mexican counterparts had longed served as rowdy
forums for political discussion and agitation that sometimes spilled into the street in armed conflict or political
protest. The Inn of San Felipe seems to fit this description. In the early 1800s, while billeted at the inn, insur-
gent colonel Father Pablo Calvillo orchestrated the
rebellion against the Spanish Crown in Jalisco.

The San Felipe wasn't the only inn with a political
past. On the night of June 26, 1880, a mob of eight hundred radical liberals gathered in and about a place called
the New World Inn to celebrate the defeat of the conservative candidate for governor. Emboldened by the
presence of federal troops dispatched to persuade the cit-
izenry to accept the election results, the mob took to the
streets shouting "Vivas!" for the winner and "Death!"
to the loser, provoking a rash of fights that left two dead
and eight wounded by the morning.

Whatever side Antonio joined, Gregorio recalls that
his brother's departure provided him with a job: "I took
charge of the Inn, substituting for my brother Antonio
because he had dedicated himself to the armed services."
Gregorio's chronicle next turns its attention to his
courtship of Trinidad, a prosaic account of births and baptisms, and then the siege of Guadalajara: "In this year, a
notable event occured, the final siege of Guadalajara,
which began the 25th of September. There was a very
bitter attack under the command of General Zaragoza

[who later repulsed the French at the Battle of Puebla on May 5, 1862]." Gregorio notes that Zaragoza had taken charge of the siege because Don Jesus G. Ortega, the commander in charge of the liberal army in Jalisco, was stricken by malaria. As the month wore on, hunger and the spread of typhus decimated the conservative forces. After the liberals tightened their grip on the city and turned back reinforcements, "Gen. Severo Castillo, leader of the besieged forces, capitulated, thereby leaving the liberals victorious that same day, the 29th of October."

Then a mysterious gap appears. Twelve of the faintly blue pages have been neatly excised from his notebook as if with a razor. These missing pages, I suspect, held the secret of Antonio's political loyalties. Still, these family records offer enough detail to sketch a portrait of Gregorio's family. Gregorio, Trinidad, and their descendants seem typical of their social caste: the small merchants, craftsmen, and bureaucrats of Guadalajara's *mestizo* petite bourgeoisie. Nearly a half century later, elements of this former caste would emerge as a driving force behind the Revolution of 1910.

Catalina, Gregorio's and Trinidad's third child, was born on September 25, 1862. She first appears in an old, hand-painted photograph on her twelfth birthday. She comes across as fragile and distant, clothed in lengths of burgundy silk flowing to her shoes, and a violet velvet bodice buttoned up to her neck. She is photographed again four years later. She already fits the image of a proud but solitary spinster. Her pupils are dense and black, her upper lip and nose are slightly deformed. Catalina, a teacher, first taught in the elementary parochial school in nearby San Pedro Tlaquepaque,

A DAGUERREOTYPE OF TRINIDAD AND HER HUSBAND, GREGORIO, WITH TWO DAUGHTERS ON THEIR LAPS, CIRCA 1860S.

where she jotted down her recipes at age twenty-six. She was eventually transferred to the parochial school in downtown Guadalajara. She is said to have spoken French and some English, written poems, and entertained at least one impossible romance. She died in early middle age. But she is just sixteen in the photograph. In her hands she holds up a small book, probably a volume of didactic verses to indicate her scholarly inclinations, as she sits before a tapestry background resembling a lush landscape of the Tuscan woods.

Don Octaviano de la Mora, Guadalajara's first professional photographer, learned his style of posing subjects in fanciful settings in Paris after his apprenticeship with Louis Jacques Mandé Daguerre. Which explains why Don Octaviano's *salón de posiciones* was more than a setting where portraits were taken. It was a magical place where an emerging middle class invented its identity. With head cocked slightly toward the volume of verses, Catalina peers back as if wishing to tell us that her pose is its own reward; she had succeeded at fixing her decency in time.

Gregorio's birth certificate says that he was born in Juchipila, today a town situated in the highland plateaus of northeastern Jalisco. Besides lodging and feeding his guests, his job required that he let mule teams to the *arrieros* and road crews maintaining the highway to the port of Manzanillo.

Weighed down by the declining haciendas, thousands of small landowners, shopkeepers, and tradesmen sold what they had in the provinces, bought mules teams and wagons, and headed to Guadalajara. That's where the money was during the midnineteenth century, hauling goods to and from Mexico's fastest-growing city. The *arrieros* or muleteers were a lot like the Kansas or Wyoming farm boys who jumped behind the wheel of a big rig to escape their hard scrabble farms. The hauling trade brought Gregorio and his family into contact with muleteers, traveling salesmen, and assorted hustlers from all over the republic. These new immigrants brought with them their appetites for home cooking, which meant that each of Western Mexico's regional cuisines could be found in Guadalajara's inns.

WE GET A HINT OF WHAT INN COOKING WAS like from the advertisements published in Guadalajara's newspapers. The "Mexican Dinner" advertised in 1888 by one inn listed one soup, or *sopa caldosa*, one pasta dish, or *sopa seca*, eggs

RESTAURANT ADVERTISEMENT PUBLISHED IN THE 1888 EDITIONS OF *JUAN PANADERO*, A GUADALAJARA NEWSPAPER.

(any style), beefsteak, chicken, vegetables, beans, candied fruit, and a cup of coffee, all for thirty-seven *centavos*. Simple, cheap, and sensible. The basic meals were washed down with pulque, beer, or tequila.

The menu provides a basic outline of an inn-cooked meal, but not exactly *how* it was prepared. In Mexico's nineteenth-century novels, the food served at inns sometimes evoked scenes where juicy roasts of beef or lamb or game birds turned on spits, which were then removed from the smoky fire and carved for the admiring traveler, and served with fresh baked bread and home-brewed beer. At other times, the portrait of meals served in the inns summoned up images of wormy meat, transparent soups, and hard bread; or simply nothing at all before the guest turned in for the night. The truth probably lies somewhere between these two extremes.

As the newspaper advertisement shows, the inns offered a menu of simple foods prepared in simple ways, which isn't surprising. Since most of the muleteers came from the surrounding provinces, the standard fare served at an inn such as the San Felipe, we can assume, was a blend of provincial cooking and popular street food—tacos, enchiladas, and so on. Yet humble cooking didn't mean sameness or blandness. Guadalajara straddled several regional cultures and climatic zones, and so it drew upon a variety of cooking styles and ingredients; highland wheat and corn, lowland sugarcane and pineapple, freshwater fish and saltwater shrimp.

Trinidad's culinary knowledge should also be factored into the mix. As a girl raised in her mother's boardinghouse, she had firsthand knowledge about running a busy kitchen and filling up the greatest number of bellies at the least expense. Her recipes provide indirect evidence of this. Hers were mostly day-to-day recipes that she drew upon to feed a large family and the guests who stayed at the San Felipe. No doubt her husband sought her advice, a relationship that must have been reflected in his menu. He was probably free—within the limits of popular taste—to serve some of what his guests requested, and some of what Trinidad suggested.

Influenced by the provinces, street fare, and the recipes she inherited from her mother, the following dishes represent a sampling of what she might have heaped on the inn's coarse plank tables for a half-dozen hungry mule drivers.

Puchero

Unfortunately, there's one ingredient from Catalina's kitchen you can't buy off the shelf—that's her all-purpose soup broth. No decent sauce, soup, stew, or mole can be made without a good Mexican-style soup broth called *puchero*. Whole chickens, joints of lamb, veal, or ham emerged steaming from the *puchero*-filled kettle to be heaped on one platter, while vegetables and garbanzos were arranged on another.

As important as the broth was to the family's cooking, neither my Aunt Catalina nor her mother bothered to jot down a recipe. They didn't have to. They'd already memorized it. *Puchero* differs from present-day beef stocks since it requires combinations of meats, such as pork and beef, or veal and lamb, grains such as rice or garbanzos, and generous amounts of herbs and aromatic vegetables. Canned beef stock just can't duplicate a good *puchero*'s mellower, more aromatic flavors. Our version was adapted from Alicia Leo's recipe in *Cuaderno de recetas de Doña Josefita Gordoa y Ortíz: Año de 1846* (Recipe Notebook of Madame Josefita Gordoa y Ortiz de Rozas: Year of 1846).

2 quarts cold water
2 pounds sliced beef shank with bones
½ pound chicken (skin removed optional)
½ cup precooked garbanzo beans
1 medium white onion, halved
1 large garlic clove
2 medium carrots, peeled and halved
1 medium turnip, peeled and halved
1 medium parsnip, peeled and cut into
    large pieces
1 bay leaf
½ teaspoon whole white peppercorns
½ teaspoon salt
4–5 whole stems Italian parsley
1 medium summer squash, zucchini, or chayote,
    quartered

Optional: One other vegetable, such as string beans, fresh corn, potatoes, or cabbage.

PREPARATION

In a 10-quart kettle, add the cold water, beef shank, chicken, and garbanzos. (You can prevent the garbanzos from rolling about by wrapping them inside a small cheesecloth sack and then dangling the sack in the broth like a teabag. The large, two-sided perforated metal canisters sold in Mexico for this purpose are also effective.) Add onion, garlic, carrots, turnip, parsnip, bay leaf, peppercorns, salt, and parsley. Slowly bring the broth to a boil. Reduce heat and cook covered for 1-½ hours. Add squash and optional vegetables 15 minutes before serving. Remove vegetables and meat from pot and serve the meat on one platter and the vegetables and garbanzos on another. (See next recipe for more options.) Strain the broth and cool it in the refrigerator for at least 1 hour. Skim away fat that floated to the surface with a spoon. This recipe makes 5-½ cups of broth, or enough for the soups featured in this book.

SERVES 6 TO 8

A One-Kettle Feast

Puchero is good for more than its broth. A well-seasoned kettle of it can make a classy sit-down feast in a matter of minutes. Serve the cooked meats and vegetables from a platter while they're still hot. Then strain the broth, reheat it, pour it into a tureen, and quickly garnish with the following fresh herbs:

⅓ cup finely chopped mint
⅓ cup finely chopped *cilantro*
⅓ cup finely chopped Italian parsley

Serving hint: A tureen and soup bowls of clear glass will show off the green herbs in the steamy broth. A simple lettuce salad dressed in olive oil and vinegar, a hot baguette or some steamy tortillas, and a side dish of pickled jalapeños will complete this meal quite nicely.

Sopa de Garbanzo

Garbanzo Soup

In this recipe, the humble, wholesome garbanzo is dressed up in a broth of astonishing sweet and sour flavors. It was one of several garbanzo soups handed down in my family. My mother learned this version from my father, who learned it from his mother. It has the added virtue of being a Mexican specialty that tastes equally authentic with fresh or canned ingredients.

4 tablespoons olive oil
1 medium yellow onion, diced
2 garlic cloves, minced
1 cup tomatoes, roasted, peeled, and pureed
4 cups chicken broth
2 15-ounce cans garbanzo beans, drained
4 pickled yellow chiles or *tornachiles*
5 tablespoons fresh or canned pineapple juice
5 slices fresh or canned pineapple in
    sweet syrup cut into chunks (reserve syrup)
5 sprigs fresh oregano, minced, or ½ teaspoon
    dry oregano
½ teaspoon salt
1 teaspoon sugar (optional)

PREPARATION
Heat the olive oil in a 12-inch skillet over a medium flame. Sauté the onions and garlic for about 2 minutes, or until the onions become almost translucent. Add the tomato and allow it to sizzle 1 minute longer, then add the chicken broth, garbanzos, pickled chiles, pineapple juice, pineapple chunks and syrup, oregano, and salt, and simmer for 5 minutes. (Add 1 teaspoon sugar to soup if fresh or unsweetened canned pineapple is used.) Serve hot or cold with hot crusty sourdough bread. SERVES 5 TO 6

Sopa de Tortilla

Tortilla Casserole

Imagine spicy ham-sausage-tomato sauce layered between palm-size tortillas packed with chunks of salty, crumbly *cotija* cheese. But remember, you'll have to resist the temptation to eat the steamy tortillas before they make it to the casserole. So double the dough recipe, bake extra tortillas, and nibble on them while you assemble the dish.

1 cup Quaker Oats Masa Harina de Maíz
    (corn tortilla mix)
½ cup warm water
1 cup grated *cotija* cheese
1–2 tablespoons water (optional)
5 tablespoons olive oil
1 tablespoon butter
1 teaspoon finely ground dry Mexican oregano
1-¼ cups tomatoes, roasted, peeled,
    and chopped
½ cup chopped ham
¾ cup crumbled *longaniza* sausage, fried
    and drained
½ cup chopped yellow onions
12 inches wax paper

PREPARATION

Mix the prepared *masa* with warm water and grated cheese in a large mixing bowl, then knead until the *masa*, or cornmeal dough, is thoroughly moist, but not pasty. Knead in 1 or 2 tablespoons of water if the dough is too crumbly. Take about 2 tablespoons of dough and roll it in your palms into a walnut-size ball. Place the dough ball between two pieces of wax paper inside the press, and make a tortilla. The tortilla should be about 3 inches in diameter.

Heat 2 tablespoons olive oil and 1 tablespoon butter in a 10-inch skillet over a medium flame. Sauté each tortilla for 30 seconds on each side. Repeat this procedure, making about a dozen or more. Use additional oil and butter as needed.

Heat the remaining 3 tablespoons olive oil in another 10-inch skillet over a medium flame. Add 1 teaspoon Mexican oregano and tomatoes, then sauté for 1 minute. Add ham, *longaniza*, and onions. Sauté for another 2 minutes.

Preheat oven to 350 degrees. Place a layer of tortillas at the bottom of an attractive 12-inch, ovenproof casserole, then add a layer of the filling over the tortillas. Repeat the layering process. Top with a final layer of filling and 2 tablespoons *cotija* cheese. Bake the casserole for 20 minutes. Serve hot.
SERVES 6

Coles Endiablados

Deviled Cabbage

2 medium *chiles anchos*, washed, seeded,
  and deveined
1 cup hot water
4 large garlic cloves, roasted, peeled,
  and minced fine
3 cups water
1 large white cabbage, quartered
½ cup olive oil
⅓ cup white wine vinegar
1 teaspoon salt
1 teaspoon dried Mexican oregano

PREPARATION

Heat a heavy skillet over a medium flame and sauté chiles for 30 seconds or until skins turn dark red. Soak the toasted *ancho* chile skins in 1 cup hot water for 2 hours. Place the *ancho* skins, garlic, and ½ cup soaking solution in blender and process to a smooth paste with soaking solution from the chiles. Pour the paste into a bowl and set aside. Bring 3 cups water to a boil in a Dutch oven or heavy stockpot with a tight-fitting lid. Add the cabbage and blanch over a medium flame for 5 minutes. Do not let the cabbage get too soft. Remove the cabbage and drain in a colander. Save the cabbage broth. When cool, coarsely chop the cabbage and place it in a large mixing bowl. Add 1 cup of the reserved cabbage broth, ½ cup *ancho* paste, olive oil, vinegar, salt, and hand-crumbled oregano. Gently toss the salad and taste. You may wish to add more salt, oregano, or *ancho* paste. Refrigerate the salad 2 hours before serving. SERVES 6

Otra Torta Cacera

Another Home-Style Frittata

2 ears fresh sweet corn, yellow or white
3 tablespoons olive oil
2 garlic cloves, minced fine
½ cup diced onions
2 tablespoons chopped Italian parsley
5 large eggs
⅛ teaspoon salt
5 chiles verdes, roasted, sweated, and peeled,
    cut into thin strips
½ cup grated *cotija* cheese or Romano cheese

PREPARATION

Remove the husk and silk from each ear of corn and rinse. Stand the ear on its wide end at an angle perpendicular to the cutting board, and slice the kernels away from the ear without cutting into the cob itself. Repeat the process for each ear and set the kernels aside. Preheat broiler. Heat olive oil in a 12-inch skillet over a medium flame. Sauté the garlic, onions, corn kernels, and 1 tablespoon Italian parsley for 3 to 4 minutes. In a large bowl, beat the eggs and salt with a fork. Pour the eggs over the sautéed vegetables and allow them to set, cooking for 3 to 4 minutes. Carefully run spatula around edge, lifting the beaten eggs to let the uncooked egg mixture flow underneath. Top the *torta* with the remaining 1 tablespoon parsley, green chile strips, and grated cheese. Place the skillet under the broiler at maximum heat for about 2 minutes, or until the *torta* develops a nice, golden crust. Remove the torta, and slice and serve hot. SERVES 4 TO 5

Bif Stec

Grilled Steak

4 tablespoons minced garlic
1 tablespoon coarsely ground black
   peppercorns
1 teaspoon salt
5 Mexican limes or 2 lemons, juiced
3 pounds skirt steaks, sliced into 6 servings
½ cup bay leaves

PREPARATION

Place the garlic, peppercorns, salt, and lime juice in a food processor or a *molcajete* and grind to a coarse paste. Place the steaks in a small roasting pan and baste the steaks on all sides with the marinade.

   Place the steaks on a large platter and cover with about 6 bay leaves on each side. Stack the steaks on top of one another in a large bowl, add any leftover marinade, and cover with plastic wrap. Marinate the steaks in the refrigerator for 4 hours. Remove and discard the bay leaves before grilling or broiling the steaks, but not if you intend to barbecue them; the burned bay leaves add to the flavor.

SERVES 6

Pollos Borrachos

Drunken Chickens

Some food historians trace this recipe to Aguascalientes, an inland state that neighbors Jalisco. The Aguascalientes version stews the chicken in *pulque*, an alcoholic drink made from the century plant. Trinidad cooked hers with sherry, a practical and delicious alternative. But a word of caution: The *chorizon* is a spicy pork sausage tied off in short, fat links. Avoid buying prepackaged *chorizos* sold in supermarkets. Usually these sausages are incorrectly seasoned and stuffed with unmentionable meat by-products. Instead, find a neighborhood *tortillería*, Mexican butcher shop, or Hispanic *bodega*, and ask for aged *chorizones*. These maroon-colored sausages are firm, not mushy like most supermarket brands. If real Mexican-style *chorizones* aren't available, ask for Spanish-style *chorizo*, or Mexican *longaniza*, a longer pork sausage that you can cut into two-inch-long pieces.

¼ cup peanut oil
1 large chicken, quartered
½ pound ham, cut into ¼-inch-thick strips
½ pound whole *chorizones*, cut into
    individual links
1 teaspoon finely minced garlic
½ teaspoon black pepper
½ teaspoon nutmeg
5 whole cloves, ground coarse
½ teaspoon salt
2 cups tomato, roasted and pureed
1 cup dry sherry

GARNISH
Green olives
Pickled serrano chiles

PREPARATION
Heat the oil in a 12-inch skillet over a high
flame for 3 minutes, then reduce heat to
medium. Carefully place the quartered chicken
in the pan and sauté until golden. Remove
and drain on paper towels. Pour 2 tablespoons
oil from the skillet into an 8-quart Dutch oven
or heavy stewing pot and heat it over a
medium flame. Sauté the ham, *chorizones*,
garlic, and spices for 4 minutes. Add the salt,
chicken, tomatoes, and sherry. Bring to
a boil, reduce heat to low, cover with
a tight-fitting lid, and simmer for 45 minutes.
Serve on a platter and garnish with green
olives and pickled serrano chiles.
SERVES 6 TO 7

the hidden garden

T RINIDAD AND CATALINA'S CULINARY lives revolved around two spaces separated by more than distance: The San Felipe, a semipublic space opened to the world, and Trinidad's household, a private place reserved for friends and family. Both spaces filled special niches within the city's social geography.

In 1888, Guadalajara was a city divided in concentric circles of decreasing wealth and increasing color. At its core was the seat of power: expansive basalt-covered plazas framed by straight rows of bushy orange trees, imposing government and church ministries and multistoried mansions owned by wealthy *criollos*, the lighter-skinned descendants of the Spanish colonists. In the circle farthest from the core survived the remnants of pre-Hispanic marketplaces such as Mexicaltzingo and the Mercado Libertad, later renamed San Juan de Dios, a magical space reclaimed by the city's first inhabitants.

"Between these Indian outskirts and the wealthy, Europeanized center," writes historian Richard Lindley, "lay a large, indeterminate district inhabited by professionals, semiprofessionals, craftsmen, shopkeepers, laborers, unemployed people, transients, beggars, mule drivers, ...soldiers, and simple hustlers whose lifestyle ran the gamut from extreme poverty to the near side of opulence."

Catalina and her parents lived and worked here, in the city's ambiguous zone between races and classes. Their nondescript homes of massive adobe walls were rarely whitewashed, and were often weathered down to crumbling clay. Unappealing and uninviting houses they seemed, at least when approached from the street. But the disregard for exterior appearances changed the moment you stepped into the shaded entryway.

At the end of a long corridor was the patio — a recuperation of private space and sunlight framed by a Moorish garden. Many of the middle zone's residents had arrived only recently, bringing with them memories of garden plots and fields and hillsides crowded with indigenous flora from nearby subtropic highlands or tropic lowlands. Guadalajara's residents planted the memories of their rural landscapes in their patios.

A typical middle-class household was built around one or two interior patios that reserved small garden plots for cultivating herbs and fruit trees. No space was wasted. Chayotes, a tropical vine squash, were trained to cling to trellises and patio walls. When planted in Guadalajara's sandy pumice soil, the vine produced a *chinchayote*, a large, edible root especially good when boiled and cooked in omelets. My Aunt Estela was most impressed by Catalina's patio. It was a large and sunny square of dark gray basalt slabs framed on all sides with rows of basalt columns. A square fountain gurgled at the patio's center, its water spilling from four spouts used for watering the patio's cauldron-size clay planters. Some, placed halfway under the shaded porticos, were lush with parsley, thyme, marjoram, oregano; others, planted with lime and lemon trees, were stationed in full sun. The *azoteas*, or sun roofs of Guadalajara's rambling adobe houses, became platforms for chicken coops. Pigeons, which fulfilled the roles of pets and a reserve food supply, could be raised up there, too, in a specially built dovecote. Hogs or turkeys were penned in the stables at the rear of the house along with a cow or pair of nanny goats that supplied the milk.

The following recipes suggest the kind of homegrown meal Trinidad or Catalina could have improvised from what they found in their chicken coop and garden.

Sopa de Gallina

Chicken Soup

Although Catalina's recipe was designed for the older hen pecking about her patio, it's certainly not an ordinary chicken soup.

BROTH

6 quarts cold water
1 large, whole chicken (at least 4 pounds), discard innards
3-½ pounds beef bones
2 medium white onions, quartered
3 medium turnips, peeled and quartered
3 medium carrots, peeled and halved
1 tablespoon coarsely chopped garlic
1 cup garbanzos (soaked overnight)
1 teaspoon salt

Slowly bring all the ingredients to a boil in an 8-quart kettle, cover, and simmer 45 minutes, or until chicken is thoroughly cooked. Remove the chicken from the broth, cut away the breast meat and cube about 1-½ cups for the soup. Strain 5 cups of broth. Place the broth in the refrigerator and allow to cool for a half hour. Skim the fat that has risen to the surface. Set meat and broth aside.

SOUP

2 tablespoons olive oil
½ medium white onion, chopped fine
1 tablespoon finely minced garlic
1 large ripe tomato, chopped fine
¼ teaspoon white pepper
⅛ teaspoon freshly ground nutmeg
½ teaspoon salt, or to taste
5 cups strained broth
1-½ cups cooked chicken meat, cubed
2 large egg yolks, hard-cooked
¼ cup very dry sherry

Heat 2 tablespoons olive oil in a heavy 3- to 4-quart saucepan over a medium flame. Sauté the onions and garlic about 2 minutes or until they begin to appear translucent. Raise the heat and add the tomato; sauté another 5 minutes, stirring to prevent burning. Season with white pepper, nutmeg, and salt. Add 5 cups strained broth and simmer for 10 minutes over a medium flame, or until the flavors blend. You may choose to add an extra pinch of pepper or nutmeg at this point to adjust the flavors.

Using a fine sieve, strain mixture into another bowl, gently pressing the tomato and onion with the back of a wooden spoon. Return the strained soup to the saucepan and simmer. Add the cubed chicken. Remove about ½ cup of soup from the saucepan and slowly pour into a small bowl with the hard-cooked yolks, whisking constantly until smooth. Return the yolk-broth mixture to the saucepan. Stir in dry sherry and serve hot. SERVES 5 TO 6

Chayotes en Adobo

Chayotes and Pork in Adobo Sauce

3 teaspoons olive oil
2 medium *chiles anchos*, destemmed, deveined, and seeded
1 dried *chilaca* or New Mexico chile, destemmed, deveined, and seeded
1 teaspoon white wine vinegar
2-½ cups warm water (reserve ¾ cup soaking solution)
1 teaspoon salt
⅓ cup toasted sesame seeds (reserve 1 tablespoon for garnish)
3–4 large chayotes
2 quarts water
1 pound pork shoulder
1 cup water
1 large bay leaf
1 cup homemade or canned chicken broth
1 cup chayote broth
1 large garlic clove
¼ cup crumbled *cotija* cheese

Pan toast the chiles in 1 teaspoon oil, then soak them in a medium mixing bowl with 1 teaspoon vinegar and 2-½ cups warm water for 1 hour. Reserve ¾ cup soaking solution. After soaking, place the chile skins in a blender with ½ cup soaking solution, then add salt and all but 1 tablespoon of the toasted sesame seeds. Blend to a smooth paste. Add ¼ cup soaking solution if chiles will not blend to a smooth texture.

Meanwhile, simmer the chayotes in a covered 5-quart kettle with 2 quarts water over a medium flame for 45 minutes. Remove the chayotes, cool, peel, and chop into 1-½-inch cubes. Set aside.

Place the pork in a 3-quart pot with 1 cup water, 1 bay leaf, 1 cup chicken broth, 1 cup chayote broth, 1 garlic clove, and simmer over a low flame for 20 minutes. Remove the meat and chop into bite-size pieces. Strain 2 cups pork broth, and set aside.

Heat 2 teaspoons oil in a 12-inch skillet over a medium flame. Add the chile paste and sauté, stirring constantly to prevent sticking. Pour in 2 cups pork broth, 4 cups cubed chayote, 1-½ cups chopped pork. Cover and simmer for 10 minutes. Garnish each serving with a pinch of crumbled *cotija* cheese and a pinch of sesame seeds. SERVES 5 TO 6

violent consommé:

the making of a mestizo cuisine

"TOAST, DEVEIN, AND SAUTÉ EQUAL POR-tions of *pasilla* and *ancho* chiles," Trinidad's daughter, Catalina, writes, naming the wrinkled, vanilla-colored pods used in making mole sauces. "Then toast the seeds of the same chiles and grind them with peanuts, clove, and cinnamon . . ."

So begins her first recipe—something she called *mole caraqueño de carnero*, or lamb mole Caracas-style.

As recipes go, the meaning and purpose of these instructions may seem remote, buried in distant culinary history. Followed closely, how-ever, old recipes allow us the impossible: to sit down with ghosts and taste a mole as savored by relatives or strangers at a Sunday lunch prepared by my great-great-aunt Catalina in 1888. But a meal with the dead calls for a few introductions.

Catalina's mole belongs to a family of sauces—some brilliant yellow, others green, red, or almost black—dating back to pre-Hispanic times. In time, the family divided into more than a half-dozen branches. Mole-like sauces such as *man-chamanteles*, literally the tablecloth stainers, *pipi-anes*, pumpkin-seed-based sauces, or the *clemoles*, the tomato-based sauces, represent a few off-shoots, each blending a different combination of seeds, spices, fruits, and fresh or dried chiles. Catalina's recipe, though simple compared to oth-ers calling for dozens of ingredients, wonder-fully enhances the flavors of lamb, then a favorite of middle-class families living in central and west-ern cities such as Mexico City and Guadalajara.

She probably copied her recipe word for word from the 1853 edition of *Novísimo Arte De Cocina o Colección de Las Mejores Recetas* (The Latest Art of Cooking or Collection of the Best Recipes), pub-lished by Simón Blanquel. After more digging, we found that all of Catalina's recipes were, if not word-for-word copies, then ingredient-by-ingredient duplicates of recipes published in books such as Blanquel's. The influence of European cuisine, particularly French culinary fashions, might lead one to conclude that the published recipes were essentially derivative, and thus not authentically Mexican. However, a careful reading of these recipes reveals the cuisine's true origins.

Like so much of American cookery, most Mexican cookbook recipes are hybrids. Some are European recipes redesigned for Mexican tastes. Others reverse the process—indigenous ingredients and recipes subjected to European cooking styles. Even the so-called European roots of Mexican cookery are not exactly what they appear to be. The pastrylike breads made from garbanzos betray Moroccan origins; the walnut and almond sauces decorated with pomegranate seeds are Arabic standards, while the fragrant methods of pickling vegetables, fish, and poultry called *escabeches* can be traced to Persia. In any case, whether by deliberate choice or accidental discovery, a new cuisine was being created. Still, full recognition of this new cuisine did not come until four centuries after the conquest, when Mexico proclaimed its independence from Spain and took over the printing presses the Spaniards had controlled for centuries. With their new freedoms, publishers such as Blanquel set out to express their national identity. After centuries of seeing their cuisine ignored, they published the first cookbooks containing recipes like Catalina's mole.

During the sixteenth, seventeenth, and eighteenth centuries, very few *criollo*, or New World–born Spanish housewives, wrote down the recipes created by their servants, the Indians, Africans, and *mestizos*, or the people created from a mixture of Europeans and Indians. With the important exception of nuns, reading and writing were privileges rarely extended to women in New Spain prior to the nineteenth century. As time passed, however, a contradiction emerged. While the upper classes publicly professed a love of European cooking, especially during public ceremonial occasions, the food they craved in private was distinctly *mestizo*. At such moments a housewife may have turned to a rare family cookbook such as the notebook of recipes jotted down by the housekeeper of Doña María Dolores Calderón in 1829, one of the earliest of Mexico's private recipe collections.

Other factors contributed to culinary *mestizaje*, or the cultural fusion that began when the first Europeans stumbled into the Americas. First came the incalculable suffering of conquest. It is estimated that as many as fourteen million indigenous persons perished in New Spain by 1570. Those who survived were virtually enslaved. Paradoxically, after having pulled them to the brink of extinction, the Spanish crown next moved to ensure the survival and eventual recovery of indigenous populations, also thus ensuring the survival of many indigenous cultivars and methods of cultivation—the foundations of pre-Hispanic cuisine. Meanwhile, in the midst of all this death and subjugation, New Spain became the stage of an equally far-reaching cultural drama. During the sixteenth and seventeenth centuries, the baroque search for ever more exotic artistic effects made the dominant Spanish culture susceptible to New World influences. In such a climate, culinary experimentation married Mediterranean, European, native, African, and Asian influences. The convents of New Spain deserve special credit for consecrating many, but by no means all, of these culinary marriages.

That cuisine has evolved into what most Mexicans would recognize today, a *mestizo* cuisine. This mixing produced several regional cuisines. Though different, each expresses its violent origins in conquest with stunning sensual juxtapositions. Every culinary effect is calculated to intensify flavors and excite the eye. Unlike traditional Spanish food, a cuisine for which appearances have been less important, the ancient Mexican love of decoration reveals an affinity to Chinese culinary design. The indigenous eye thrives upon intriguing disguises. Think of the moles, which transform ordinary hens into radiant pheasants. And *mestizo* cookery is boldly unpuritanical. Mexico's poet laureate, Octavio Paz, writes that Mexican cooking prefers the "shock of tastes; cool and piquant, salt and sweet, hot and tart, pungent and delicate. Desire is the active agent, the secret producer of changes, whether it be in transition from one flavor to another or the contrast between several. In gastronomy as in the erotic, it's desire that sets substances in motion; this is the power that rules their conjunction, commingling, and transmutation."

Chile, in its hundred varieties and intensities, plays a crucial role in the dialogue of desire. Whether aromatic, sweet, or incendiary, the family of species known as capsicum possesses the seemingly magical power to open taste buds to opposing flavors. A new world of taste experiences thus become possible through synchronicity: Like ancestors summoned from the earth, defeated pre-Columbian gods could momentarily possess the souls of Catholic angels through a kind of gustatory hallucination. Catalina's *mole caraqueño* thus inverts the symbolism of conquest: She used the Indian sauces to vanquish the conqueror's roast lamb. Ironically, this cuisine of sublime blasphemies was elevated to art by sixteenth-century nuns who experimented with pagan New World flavors while the Inquisition raged outside their convent walls. More than four centuries later, proper schoolmarms like Catalina passed this style on to a new generation of women.

A Sunday Lunch: Guadalajara 1888

NOT EVERY MEAL IN TRINIDAD'S HOME JUSTI-fied a seven-course feast. But compared to how we today rush to cook fast and eat even faster, meal preparation in Catalina's day was extravagantly time-consuming. And the opportunities for feasting were multiplied in a society that so strongly emphasized communal family values. Saints' days, birthdays, baptisms, weddings, engagements, coming-of-age parties, and the seemingly endless parade of religious and national holidays were all good excuses for big family feasts. And don't forget friends. Families like Catalina's were expected to set aside at least one weekday meal for their closest friends. Sunday lunches were reserved for married sons, daughters, and any family relations who might drop in after mass for a seven-course meal, including two desserts.

Orchestrating a holiday noonday meal thus required careful preparation. Like a general planning an arduous campaign, the fussier middle-class homemaker of Catalina's day may have diagrammed seating arrangements and placement of plates and silverware. Next, the family cook and servants were called into the kitchen to get their orders. Homemakers like Catalina or Trinidad usually read their recipes aloud to the cook, going over each ingredient, each procedure. This system wasn't as impractical as it sounds. Since *mestizo* and Indian girls were virtually indentured to a lifetime of cooking for one family, they were trained to memorize the household's favorite recipes. A quick review was all an experienced cook needed to refresh her memory.

After its preparation, the family feast would be served in the following courses. First came the *sopa caldosa*, literally a brothy soup, followed by *sopa seca*, which was a kind of rice, tortilla, or pasta dish to which soup stock might be added. Next came the *principio*, or opening main dish, which usually consisted of a *guisado*—a variety of stew-like dishes—or a mole. This course was followed by the *asado*, or roast, which could be garnished with an array of cooked and fresh salsas, some piquant and some not. An *ensalada guisada*, a cooked vegetable salad usually dressed in oil and a homemade fruit vinegar, followed the roast. The meal was topped off with a *postre* (dessert), *dulce* (homemade candy), or fresh fruit, and perhaps some sweet mint tea to settle their stomachs. Formal meals could be expanded to include as many as five dishes per course, as well as other introductory and intermediary courses, such as an appetizer of *chiles en frío*, or cold stuffed chiles. But that was then. We don't expect you to entertain like the Vargas family. Instead, you can experience the spirit of Catalina's Violent Consummé by mixing and matching these recipes to create a personal *mestizo* cuisine.

APERETIVOS

Chiles en Frío Rellenos de Camaron

Chiles Stuffed with Shrimp

STUFFING

1-¼ teaspoon salt
½ pound cooked, shelled, and deveined
    jumbo shrimp, chopped coarse
⅓ cup finely chopped Italian parsley
3 teaspoons minced capers
½ cup finely chopped Spanish green olives
2 tablespoons olive oil
1 tablespoon finely chopped garlic
½ cup finely chopped yellow onion
¼ teaspoon white pepper
¼ cup white wine vinegar
12 large fresh Anaheim, poblano, or New
    Mexico chiles, washed, roasted, sweated,
    peeled, and left whole (see Appendix)

MARINADE

1 cup finely diced tomato
2 tablespoons finely chopped fresh oregano
1 cup finely chopped Italian parsley
1 tablespoon finely chopped capers
1 tablespoon finely chopped green olives
½ teaspoon salt
½ cup olive oil
⅓ cup white wine vinegar

PREPARATION

To make the stuffing, mix the salt, shrimp, parsley, capers, and olives in a medium bowl, and set aside. Heat the olive oil in an 8-inch skillet over a medium flame. Sauté the garlic, onions, and white pepper until the onions become nearly translucent. Add to the shrimp mixture, then add ¼ cup of vinegar. Gently mix and set aside.

Make a 2-inch slit down from the stem end of each roasted and peeled chile (see Appendix) and carefully remove the seeds. Then gently open the slit and spoon in the shrimp stuffing, slowly but firmly pushing your finger toward the tip until it's fully stuffed. Repeat the procedure with each chile. Arrange the chiles on a platter. Set aside.

To prepare the marinade, mix tomatoes, oregano, parsley, capers, olives, and salt in a large bowl, firmly pressing the tomatoes with the back of a wooden spoon to release the juice. Blend in the oil and vinegar. Pour the marinade over the chiles, covering evenly. Serve the stuffed chiles immediately or cover and refrigerate a day before serving. SERVES 6

FIRST COURSE: SOPA CALDOSA

Consumé Violento

Violent Consommé

Catalina's recipe epitomizes the romantic sensibilities of her time. It gets its name from the manner in which an egg yolk and a dash of sherry are whisked into a tureen of steamy broth just before serving. It's important to select a very dry Spanish sherry for this recipe. Cocktail sherry is too sweet.

SOUP

2 teaspoons olive oil
1 medium white onion, quartered
1 cup roasted, peeled, and chopped tomatoes
5 cups of *puchero* broth (see p. 26)
½ teaspoon nutmeg
¼ teaspoon white pepper
1 large bay leaf
½ teaspoon salt
1 egg yolk, lightly beaten
⅛ cup dry sherry
¼ cup coarsely chopped Italian parsley

CROUTONS

3 teaspoons butter
2 teaspoons olive oil
5 slices sourdough bread cut into diamond
    shape, approximately ¾ inches in diameter

PREPARATION

Heat 1 teaspoon olive oil in an 8-inch skillet over a medium flame and sauté the onion for about 3 to 4 minutes, or until soft. Remove the onion from the skillet and, using either a food processor at the lowest speed for a few seconds, or a mortar and pestle, blend it with the roasted tomato to a pulpy texture. The sauce should not become frothy.

Heat the remaining olive oil over high heat in a medium skillet. Reduce heat to medium and add the tomato-onion mixture. The mixture should sizzle when it comes in contact with the oil. Sauté for 2 minutes. Add nutmeg, pepper, bay leaf, and salt, reduce heat, and simmer 5 minutes. Pour the tomato sauce into a large soup pot containing 5 cups of preheated broth. Bring the broth to a boil, reduce flame, and simmer for 10 minutes. Remove bay leaf.

Prepare the croutons while the broth simmers. Heat oil and butter in an 8-inch skillet over a medium flame. Add the bread and fry until golden brown. Set croutons aside.

Pour broth into a tureen and place it on the table. Immediately whisk in the beaten egg yolk, then the sherry. Serve the soup, garnishing each bowl with a pinch of parsley and a few croutons. SERVES 5 TO 6

SECOND COURSE: SOPA SECA

Sopa de Pichones
Squab on Saffron Rice

3 whole squab or quail, rinsed and halved
2 quarts water
2-½ teaspoons salt
1 tablespoon olive oil
1 medium white onion, chopped
1 garlic clove, minced
½ cup chopped Italian parsley
4 cups strained broth
2 cups long-grain rice
1 teaspoon whole Spanish saffron
¼ cup water
1-½ teaspoons cinnamon
¼ teaspoon ground clove
¼ cup white wine

GARNISH
1 large white onion, sliced into thin rings
1 cup white wine vinegar
1 teaspoon salt
1 teaspoon dry, crumbled oregano

PREPARATION
Place the squabs, 2 quarts of water, and 2 tea-spoons salt in a large kettle with a tight-fitting lid. Cover and bring to a boil. Reduce heat and simmer for 30 minutes. Heat 1 tablespoon olive oil in a skillet and sauté the onion, garlic, and parsley for 2 minutes or until the onion is nearly translucent. Turn the squabs over; add the sautéed onion, garlic, and parsley; cover and simmer another 15 minutes or until squabs are tender. Remove the squabs, strain the broth, and reserve 4 cups of broth. Set aside.

Rinse and drain the rice. Soak the saffron in ¼ cup water for 10 minutes to help the spice release its color and flavor. Pour 4 cups reserved broth, ½ teaspoon salt, saffron solution, spices, and rice into a large heavy kettle with a nonstick surface or a 13-inch paella pan with a tight-fitting lid. Bring to a boil, reduce heat to medium, and simmer uncovered for 12 minutes.

Place halved squabs over the rice. Make sure the squabs are submerged in the spiced broth solution. Pour ¼ cup white wine over the squab. Cover and simmer over low heat for another 20–25 minutes, or until rice is cooked but still moist. For the garnish, place sliced onion in a bowl. Add vinegar, salt, and crumbled oregano. Stir gently to coat the onions in vinegar. Allow to marinate 10 minutes before serving.

Serve halved squab over a bed of rice. Garnish with marinated onion rings. SERVES 6

THIRD COURSE: VERDURAS

Chicharos en Manchamanteles

Peas in Tablecloth-Staining Sauce

A smoky piquancy and cinnamon flavor is enhanced in this recipe by *piloncillo*, a form of raw sugar sold in hard, 1- to 3-ounce cones in supermarkets throughout the Southwest and in Mexican grocery stores nationwide. Dark brown sugar is a suitable substitute for *piloncillo*.

1 teaspoon olive oil
2 chile ancho pods, washed, seeded,
    and deveined
1 cup warm water
1 teaspoon white wine vinegar
1 1-inch cinnamon stick or 1 teaspoon
    ground cinnamon
3 whole black peppercorns
3 whole cloves
½ teaspoon *piloncillo*, or brown sugar
3 tablespoons olive oil
1 cup roasted, peeled, and crushed tomatoes
2 tablespoons finely ground day-old sourdough
    bread crumbs*
2 cups homemade or canned chicken broth
4 cups frozen baby peas or fresh peas
½ teaspoon salt

PREPARATION

Heat olive oil in a heavy skillet over a medium flame and sauté chiles for 30 seconds or until skins turn dark red. Soak for at least 1 hour in 1 cup warm water and 1 teaspoon vinegar. Grind skins and ½ cup soaking solution to a smooth paste in a blender (see Appendix). Pour the ancho paste into a bowl and set aside. Rinse blender with 1 or 2 tablespoons of water and save the remaining ancho paste. Grind cinnamon, peppercorns, and cloves to a powder in a *molcajete* or in an electric or manual coffee grinder reserved for spice grinding. Set aside. Place a *piloncillo* cone inside a plastic sandwich bag and crush with a mallet until pulverized. Measure ½ teaspoon of *piloncillo* and set aside. Store the remaining pulverized *piloncillo*.

    Heat 3 tablespoons olive oil in a 12-inch skillet over a high flame. Sauté the spices long enough to smell their aroma, then pour in chile ancho paste, *piloncillo*, tomatoes, and bread crumbs. Simmer 2 minutes over medium heat, stirring constantly to prevent sauce from sticking. Add the chicken broth and simmer another 5 minutes. Add the peas and salt. Fresh peas take about 6 minutes to cook, frozen peas take about 10 minutes.

    *To grind sourdough bread into crumbs, run blender at high speed and drop a few pieces of bread in at a time. SERVES 6

FOURTH COURSE: PRINCIPIO

Godornices Guisadas

Stewed Quails

2 teaspoons toasted flour
½-inch cinnamon stick or ½ teaspoon
    ground cinnamon
4 whole cloves or ¼ teaspoon ground clove
1 teaspoon salt
½ teaspoon white pepper
3 teaspoons finely minced garlic
6 tablespoons olive oil
¾ cup finely diced white onion
3 quail or Cornish game hens
    with innards, halved
1 tablespoon broth
1 cup white wine
½ cup *puchero* (see p. 26) or chicken broth
6 sprigs Italian parsley for garnish

PREPARATION

To toast flour, place in an iron skillet and brown at a low flame, stirring constantly until golden. Set aside. (You may brown a cup of flour ahead of time and store in a glass jar with a tight-fitting lid in the refrigerator).

Grind the cinnamon stick and cloves in a mortar and pestle or food processor to a fine powder (see Appendix). Add ½ teaspoon salt, pepper, and 2 teaspoons garlic and grind to the consistency of a smooth paste. Set aside.

Heat the olive oil in a 14-inch skillet over a medium flame until hot. Sauté the onions with remaining 1 teaspoon garlic for 1 minute. Add the halved birds and innards. Continue sautéeing for another 5 minutes. After meat is well sautéed, turn the flame off, remove the innards to another bowl and allow the birds to cool in the skillet.

Carefully remove all the meat from the neck bones. Place the neck meat, gizzards, 1 tablespoon chicken broth, and ground spices in a blender or food processor. Grind mixture to the consistency of a pâté. Set aside.

Reheat the birds in the skillet over a medium flame. Add the innard-spice pâté to the skillet, stirring gently for 3 minutes. Add wine, remaining salt, and continue stirring for another 3 minutes.

Dissolve the toasted flour in ½ cup of broth. Pour mixture into the skillet with the pâté and birds, stirring gently until well blended. Reduce heat to low, cover, and simmer for 25 minutes. Baste occasionally.

To serve, place halved quail on a plate and cover with enough sauce. Garnish with a sprig of Italian parsley. SERVES 6

FIFTH COURSE: ASADO

Asado de Carnero

Roast Lamb

The mole sauce, which blends vivid chiles, cinnamon, and toasted nut flavors, is unabashedly tongue-tingling. You may make each recipe separately or combine them if you have the energy to pull off the full production. A simple roast leg of lamb will suffice for a scaled-down version of Catalina's *mole caraqueño*.

ROAST
1-½ quarts water
1 6-pound leg of lamb
2 cups dry white wine
1 Mexican lime, or ½ lemon,
    cut into thin slices
2 large garlic cloves
2 teaspoons dry thyme
1 teaspoon dry oregano
2 large bay leaves
1 teaspoon whole black peppercorns
¼ cup lard
3 tablespoons olive oil
6 large garlic cloves, minced
2 teaspoons salt

PREPARATION
Preheat oven to 350 degrees. Pour 1-½ quarts water into a 10-quart kettle or one that is wide enough to hold the entire leg of lamb. Add the lamb, wine, lime or lemon slices, garlic cloves, thyme, oregano, bay leaves, and peppercorns and bring to a boil. Cover and simmer for 5 minutes over a medium flame, then turn the lamb over and simmer 5 minutes longer. Stop cooking and allow the lamb to sit in the marinade for 1 hour. Remove lamb and drain, but reserve the broth.

In a large skillet, heat the lard and olive oil over a high flame. Sauté the minced garlic and salt until golden, and set aside. Place lamb in a roasting pan and baste it with the hot garlic-oil. Roast the lamb uncovered for 55 minutes.

Remove lamb. The meat should be pink inside. Slice and serve with the following mole sauce. SERVES 6 TO 7

FIFTH COURSE: MOLE

Mole Caraqueño

Caracas-Style Lamb Mole

5 tablespoons olive oil
4 *chile ancho* pods, washed, seeded, and
    deveined (reserve seeds)
4 *chile negro* (also called *pasilla*) pods, washed,
    seeded, and deveined (reserve seeds)
2 cups hot water (reserve ½ cup soaking
    solution)
1 corn tortilla
2 teaspoons freshly ground cinnamon
½ cup raw peanuts
1 teaspoon ground clove
3 cups lamb marinade or *puchero* broth
    (see p. 26)
Salt to taste

GARNISHES
1 large red onion
½ cup white wine vinegar
½ teaspoon salt
2 large bunches radishes, washed and stemmed
1 bunch *cilantro*, rinsed
¼ cup toasted sesame seeds

PREPARATION

To prepare mole, heat 1 tablespoon olive oil in a heavy skillet over a high flame. Sauté chiles for 30 seconds or until skins turn a dark red. Soak the chile skins in 2 cups of warm water for at least 1 hour. To thoroughly submerge chiles, place a small plate over them. In a blender or food processor, blend the chile skins to a smooth paste with ½ cup or more soaking solution, and set aside. Rinse the blender with 1 tablespoon of soaking solution to retrieve any of the chile paste left behind (see Appendix). Toast the chile seeds in a heavy skillet over a medium flame until they turn a cinnamon color. You may add a few drops of oil to speed up the toasting process. Be careful not to burn the seeds as they will taste bitter. Remove the seeds and grind them thoroughly in a blender, electric coffee grinder, or a *molcajete*. Measure out 1 teaspoon ground chile seeds. Store the rest in a glass jar in the refrigerator. Set aside.

    Cut the tortilla in wedges and sauté in the same skillet in 1 tablespoon oil until they turn an even brown color. Coarsely grind the toasted tortilla wedges and set aside.

CONTINUED ON NEXT PAGE ☞

Heat 1 tablespoon oil in a 12-inch skillet over a medium flame. Sauté the ground cinnamon, peanuts, and clove for 1 minute, stirring continuously to prevent burning. Add the ground tortilla and ground chile seeds and sauté 1 minute longer while stirring. Add 1 cup chile paste and 1 cup broth and sauté vigorously for another 1 minute.

Pour contents into a blender and grind to a smooth paste. Strain mixture into a bowl by pushing the sauce through a fine sieve with the back end of a large spoon. Transfer pulp to blender with ½ cup broth and grind again. Repeat the straining process with 1 cup broth, pushing mixture through the sieve.

Heat 1 tablespoon oil over a medium flame in a 12-inch skillet, slowly pouring and stirring the mole sauce so that it sizzles on contact with the oil. Reduce heat to low. Add salt to taste and ½ cup broth. Add a few tablespoons of surplus chile paste if the mole isn't piquant enough, cover, and simmer for 15 minutes at low heat, stirring occasionally. Do not overcook the mole because it will turn a disagreeable muddy gray-brown.

GARNISH

To make the garnishes, slice the onions into thin rings, separate them, and place in a bowl with the vinegar and salt. Marinate the onion rings 30 minutes before serving.

Slice the radishes into rosettes, and place them in a large bowl filled with enough water and a half-dozen ice cubes to cover. Soak radishes for 30 minutes before serving.

Serving Instructions: Place two slices of hot roast lamb in the center of a dinner plate and cover with ¼ cup hot mole sauce. Place three rings of pickled onion over the meat and sprinkle with ½ teaspoon toasted sesame seeds. Place 1 *cilantro* sprig and 1 radish rosette opposite each other around the sauce. Repeat this garnish for each serving.

SIXTH COURSE: ENSALADAS GUISADAS

Ensalada de Chayote

Chayote Salad

This recipe's key ingredient is the chayote, or tropical vine squash, a light, lime-colored, pear-shaped vegetable with a delicate taste that's reminiscent of the Chinese winter melon, but with a subtle nut flavor. In New Orleans it is called a meliton. Its growing popularity has taken the chayote to supermarkets far beyond the Southwest.

4 large chayotes
½ medium white onion, sliced thinly
1 tablespoon olive oil
3 garlic cloves, minced
4 whole black peppercorns, crushed
2 teaspoons fresh lime juice
⅓ cup olive oil
¼ cup white wine vinegar
1 teaspoon fresh Mexican oregano,
    or ½ teaspoon dry oregano
1 teaspoon salt
4 sprigs Italian parsley

PREPARATION

Rinse the chayotes, place them in a large kettle, and pour in enough water to cover. Bring to a boil, cover, and simmer for 30 minutes. (The chayotes should feel firm when stabbed with a fork.) Remove and cool for 15 minutes, then peel with a sharp paring knife and slice into round ¼-inch- to ⅓-inch-thick slices. Arrange the chayote slices on a large platter in an attractive circular pattern. Decorate the chayotes with sliced onions.

Heat 1 tablespoon olive oil in a small saucepan over medium flame. Sauté garlic and crushed peppercorns for about 1 minute. Pour into a mixing bowl, add lime juice, ⅓ cup olive oil, vinegar, oregano, and salt while whisking briskly. Pour dressing over chayotes and decorate with Italian parsley. Serve immediately or chill for 1 hour before serving. SERVES 6

SEVENTH COURSE: POSTRE

Torta de Garbanzo

Garbanzo Torte

The cinnamon, almonds, sweetened garbanzos, and powdered sugar strongly suggest a Moorish origin to this recipe. This torte is considered a traditional favorite in Jalisco and the neighboring state of Aguascalientes.

1 pound garbanzo beans
1-½ cups vegetable shortening
1-½ cups granulated sugar
2 heaping tablespoons of Parmesan cheese or *cotija* cheese
1 tablespoon cinnamon
½ cup raisins
3 large eggs, separated

GARNISH
2–3 ounces sliced almonds
1 teaspoon confectioner's sugar

PREPARATION
Place garbanzos in a large saucepan with enough water to cover. Boil over a medium flame for 25 minutes, adding water if necessary. Drain, cool, and remove skins by gently rubbing the beans between your hands. Return beans to saucepan with enough water to cover. Boil for an additional 50 minutes, adding water if necessary. Do not overcook the garbanzos; they must be firm.

Preheat oven to 350 degrees. Drain beans and run through a hand grinder twice or mince finely in a food processor. Place in a large mixing bowl. Blend in shortening, sugar, cheese, cinnamon, and raisins. Mix in egg yolks. Whip egg whites until stiff. Fold into the mixture.

Pour into a 8"x 8"x 2" cake pan that has been precoated with butter and flour or lined with parchment paper and buttered. Sprinkle the torte with almonds. Bake for 50 minutes. Remove torte and cool before placing it on a platter.

To serve, sprinkle confectioner's sugar onto torte through a paper doily if you wish to decorate it in an elegant period style. Otherwise, sprinkle sugar over the torte through a fine sieve. SERVES 6

SEVENTH COURSE: POSTRE

Arroz Amarillo

Yellow Rice Pudding

Cinnamon, fresh orange leaves, and Jasmine-fragrant rice from Thailand make this an exotically perfumed pudding from Catalina's cookbook reminiscent of other Arab or Indian rice puddings.

⅓ cup finely ground rice, preferably the Jasmine-scented variety from Thailand, or long grain
1 cup sugar
6 cups whole milk
3 large egg yolks
2 3-inch sticks Mexican cinnamon
4 fresh orange leaves, washed, or 1 teaspoon orange extract
3 fresh orange leaves, washed, for garnish
1 orange, sliced and segmented for decoration, or canned drained mandarin oranges

PREPARATION

In a blender, put ⅓ cup dry rice and process at high speed for 10 seconds or until finely ground.

Mix ground rice, sugar, milk, and egg yolks in a 3-quart kettle. Blend thoroughly with a wire whisk. Add the cinnamon sticks and orange leaves and simmer over a low flame, stirring briskly for 25 to 30 minutes with a wire whisk to prevent sticking. Remove cinnamon sticks and orange leaves. Pour into a large platter or individual pudding dishes and cool a few minutes. Dust with ground cinnamon and decorate edges of the platter or bowls with orange slices and leaves. SERVES 8

CHAPTER FIVE

matters of taste and translation:
ancient techniques in a new world

CATALINA'S RECIPE FOR CHICKEN SOUP (PAGE 36)calls for a real's worth of soup bones. I was puzzled by her request until I learned what a *real* was. It's a Spanish coin. Its value, size, weight, and stamp varied during the more than three hundred years it circulated in New Spain. In the late eighteenth century, it traded for twenty-five centimes, or one-quarter of a Spanish *peseta*. Catalina, by using the coin, had thus resorted to the sort of shorthand measuring we use today when we ask for a quarter's worth of radishes. But how many soup bones did a *real* buy in 1888? Guadalajara old-timers say at least a pound's worth, but even they admit that this is just a guess.

The riddle of the coins illustrates one of several challenges faced in translating these recipes into modern weights and measures. It's not unusual, for example, for many of the dessert recipes to demand egg yolks by the score and sugar or lard by the pound. Obviously, modern-day concerns about nutrition and dieting didn't clutter Catalina's ideas about cooking. So we've reduced ingredient proportions, and, whenever possible, introduced healthier substitutes. But we didn't have to do all the substitutions on our own. Catalina and Trinidad helped by integrating olive oil, instead of the traditional *manteca*, or rendered pork fat, into most of their recipes. I also relied upon our best judgments and memories to interpret these recipes. Cooks like Catalina were suspicious of excessively precise measurements since recipes were meant to be interpreted.

The key exception to this rule were Catalina's candy-making methods, which required a special kind of precision. Subject headings such as "Syrup to the high pearl point" or "Syrup to the large feather point" are followed by detailed descriptions of how caramelized sugar behaves when pressed between fingertips, dipped in water, or blown into amber feathers. Catalina wasn't trying to be poetic. Since thermometers were not yet widely used in the kitchens of her day, she needed an accurate and reliable system for calibrating the numerous forms sugar takes when subjected to heat. She did this by using the ancient techniques handed down from the Arabs, who had developed a highly refined language for describing the physical properties of molten sugar. Catalina's ability to distinguish such fine gradations of texture, fragrance, and color resulted in a tremendous variety of candies, preserves, and desserts.

Her meticulous attention to detail becomes all the more remarkable when you consider her tools. Cooks today would be awed by the array of textures and flavors achieved with little more than Stone Age implements. Her food processor was the *metate*, a wide, flat basalt trough that resembles a three-legged table lowered at one end. On it, corn dough, uncooked rice, seeds, spices, raw and cooked meats were finely ground with the long, rectangular grinding stone called a *mano*, or hand. Like the *metate*, the *molcajete* is carved from basalt, but in the form of a shallow, oversized mortar. Catalina used her *molcajete* for the smaller processing jobs—grinding and mashing seeds, spices, chile, ripe avocado, and tomatoes with a four- to five-inch-long stone pestle called a *tejolote*. I have, whenever possible, substituted modern

appliances for ancient tools, but there's a reason the Mexican kitchen still reserves a place for these stone implements. A *molcajete*'s slightly porous surface, for example, grinds roasted tomatoes to that perfect pulpy texture required of both fresh and cooked sauces.

A marble mortar and wooden pestle, or heavy-duty stainless steel bowl and a big wooden ladle will do well in a pinch. The same isn't always true of electric blenders and food processors. They can, when used with a very light touch, almost duplicate the texture of tomato sauces ground in a *molcajete*. Just be careful to grind the fire-roasted tomatoes in short pulses at the slowest speeds possible. At higher grinding speeds, blenders and food processors inject too much air into the puree, which gives the sauce a horrible frothy appearance and soupy consistency. You may also find that a *molcajete* is more practical for grinding spices or toasted chile seeds. Blenders and food processors tend to scatter small quantities of spices and seeds away from the blades, which tends to shatter or splinter rather than pulverize dry spices or grains. That's why toasted chile seeds are best ground in a *molcajete* or an electric or manual coffee grinder reserved for processing spices and seeds.

Grinding ingredients in a *molcajete* requires some skill and endurance. Firing up Catalina's stove and oven required a magician's sleight of hand and a blacksmith's courage. You might call her stove a built-in, except that unlike our electric or gas-fueled contraptions, hers was a square, bench-shaped platform fashioned out of adobe blocks built out from a kitchen wall. A few of the fancier stoves were tiled, but most were just plain adobe brick. All had burnished high-fired clay stove tops perforated with several half-round fire wells called *nistencos*, which served like a gas stove's burners. A clay pot placed over a *nistenco* exposed its sooty bottom to the fire below. Wood or charcoal was loaded into the front of the stove through portals wide enough to create a good draft. If you wanted tortillas, all you had to do was place a *comal*, or clay griddle, over a *nistenco* and light a fire.

Catalina would've baked in a beehive-shaped adobe oven. Since a thermostat for gauging temperatures was out of the question, she relied upon more daring methods of temperature measurement. She risked limbs and lashes by attaching a strip of paper to the end of stick and then pointing its paper-tipped end into the oven's glowing mouth, while shielding her face with a forearm. If the paper shriveled to gold in a determined number of seconds, that indicated a particular temperature. For braver souls, the heat at which "a person's hand will not burn" indicated another temperature. And forget broilers. If you wanted a dessert or casserole with a golden crust, you simply placed a griddle over the pot or pan and placed burning embers upon the griddle. Hence Catalina's use of the term "cooked by two fires."

Essential Appliances

WHILE SOME OF CATALINA'S AND Trinidad's cooking appliances may seem antiquated, there were two in her kitchen you can't do without. One is a tortilla maker. It consists of a pair of hardwood boards or round, pot-iron plates joined at one end by hinges. When pressed together by a leverlike handle, the tortilla maker will flatten a ball of corn dough into a round disk. Place the corn dough between sheets of wax paper before pressing. The wax paper will prevent the tortilla from sticking to the tortilla maker's plates. You can find tortilla presses at most Mexican grocery stores or Latin American *bodegas*.

PEN AND INK DRAWING OF A TORTILLA PRESS, BY LUCENA VALLE

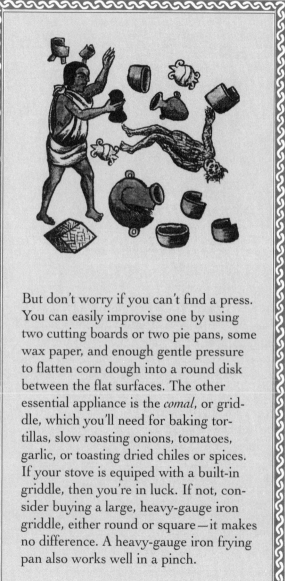

But don't worry if you can't find a press. You can easily improvise one by using two cutting boards or two pie pans, some wax paper, and enough gentle pressure to flatten corn dough into a round disk between the flat surfaces. The other essential appliance is the *comal*, or griddle, which you'll need for baking tortillas, slow roasting onions, tomatoes, garlic, or toasting dried chiles or spices. If your stove is equiped with a built-in griddle, then you're in luck. If not, consider buying a large, heavy-gauge iron griddle, either round or square—it makes no difference. A heavy-gauge iron frying pan also works well in a pinch.

IN ADDITION TO RISKY COOKING TECHNIQUES and Stone Age appliances, Catalina, like her peers, did without a refrigerator. Ever savvy, she kept a gallon-size glass jar filled with *fruta en vinagre*, or pickled fruit, which actually contained vegetables such as cauliflower and carrots in a pineapple vinegar spiced with herbs and the little yellow chiles called *tornachiles*. *Jalapeños en escabeche* was another common pickle. Fish, meat, and vegetable *escabeches*, which were perfected by the Arabs and Persians, and introduced to Mexico by the Spaniards, suffuse meaty jalapeños with an astounding array of sweet, bitter, piquant, salty, sour, and herbal flavors. In any season, gallon-size jars filled with amber liquids would perfume Catalina's kitchen. The jars were filled with a refreshing and mildly alcoholic fruit beverage called *tepache*. After further fermentation, *tepache* turns into vinegar. The most common form of *tepache* is brewed from pineapple because the naturally acidic fruit ferments so easily. But beverages brewed from other fruits are common. Although the idea of a fruit vinegar today may seem exotic—can you imagine a mango-pineapple vinegar?—these were actually a frugal homemaker's alternative to expensive bottled vinegars. Like Japanese rice vinegar, the homemade fruit vinegars are less acidic and refreshingly sweet, which means they're great for livening up salads. But don't panic. The sweeter, less acidic types of white wine or balsamic vinegar will help you to cook up reasonably authentic versions of Catalina and Trinidad's recipes.

Jalapeños en Escabeche

Pickled Jalapeños

My mother overheard this recipe as it was told to my grandmother, Delfina, by a childhood friend who learned the recipe, so the story goes, from a worker at the Clemente Jacques cannery in Guadalajara. This classic recipe uses olive oil and a fruit vinegar, which makes her jalapeños sweeter than the canned variety. But this isn't a canning recipe. It's a vegetable pickle you keep handy to spice up anything from a pizza to a sandwich. The pickled chiles will keep two months, longer if you refrigerate them.

3 pounds jalapeño chiles
1 head garlic (about 31 cloves)
1-½ cups extra virgin olive oil
2 cups peeled, sliced carrots
1 whole yellow onion, cut into slices
2 cups cauliflower florets, washed
4-½ tablespoons salt
3 tablespoons dried oregano
1 tablespoon whole black peppercorns
5 bay leaves
6 cups white wine vinegar

PREPARATIONS

Before preparing recipes, sterilize a 4 to 5 gallon glass jar by washing it thoroughly and rinsing it inside with boiling water. Turn the jar upside down to dry.

Start with the largest and freshest jalapeños you can find. Discard any damaged chiles. Remember, jalapeños that are turning red are hotter and sweeter, so you may include or discard them, according to taste. Rinse the chiles in cold water and dry them with a paper towel. Make about six little cuts in each chile with the tip of a sharp knife. This procedure will prevent expanding steam from bursting the chiles when you dunk them in hot oil. It also allows the vinegar to pickle the chiles thoroughly.

Pour the olive oil in a large stainless steel or enamel pot and heat over a medium flame, but don't allow the oil to smoke. *Caution. If you use an enamel pot, make sure it isn't chipped or cracked, as contact with metal underneath may poison the chiles. And do not use an aluminum pot.* Add the garlic cloves and chiles to the heated oil. Cook for 3 to 5 minutes, stirring to make sure the chiles are completely submerged in oil. (A shorter cooking time gives you a crisper chile.) The chiles will turn a dull color after they are cooked. Remove the pot from the fire and add the carrots, onions, cauliflower, and spices. Add the vinegar after the oil has cooled a bit to prevent it from splattering. Return the pot to the stove and heat thoroughly for another 2 minutes.

Take jar and place in it a stainless-steel knife or spoon long enough to extend beyond the jar's mouth before slowly spooning in the hot chiles, vegetables, and pickling solution. The knife absorbs the heat and prevents the jar from cracking. Use a wooden or stainless-steel spoon to transfer the *escabeche*, or pickled jalapeños and vegetables, into the jar. Allow the jar to cool before covering with a lid.

Pichones en Vinagre

Pickled Squab

This *escabeche* recipe is one of hundreds of pickled meat, fish, or vegetable recipes the Spaniards introduced to Mexico after having borrowed them from the Arabs and Persians.

2 squab or Cornish game hens
½ teaspoon salt
½ teaspoon dry thyme
1 medium white onion, sliced thin
3 whole cloves, ground
1 large bay leaf
3 garlic cloves, minced
1-½ cups white wine vinegar

Rinse the birds with cold water, pat them dry with paper towels, and rub salt and thyme on their skins and internal cavities. Place the birds breast-side up in a 6-quart Dutch oven (or large, heavy, cast-iron kettle) with a tight-fitting lid. Cover the birds with onions, cloves, bay leaf, minced garlic, and vinegar. Bring these ingredients to a boil, cover, and simmer for 25 minutes over a low flame. Turn the birds over, cover, and simmer 25 minutes longer.

Drain the birds and cool for 10 minutes. Cut the birds in halves or quarters and serve on a platter over a bed of lettuce. Decorate with the cooked onions. Serve warm or chilled.
SERVES 4

CHAPTER SIX

from holy to haute:

convent cookery in catalina's kitchen

W HAT COULD I TELL YOU, MY lady,
of the secrets of Nature which I have
discovered in cooking! That an egg
hangs together and fries in fat or oil, and that,
on the contrary, it disintegrates in syrup...
I do not wish to tire you with such trivia...
But, Madam, what is there for us women to
know, if not bits of kitchen philosophy? As
Lupercio Leonardo said: One can perfectly
well philosophize while cooking supper. And
I am always saying, when I observe these small
details: If Aristotle had been a cook, he would
have written much more.

SOR JUANA INES DE LA CRUZ from her
Reply to Sor Philothea, March 1, 1691.

RECIPES SUCH AS CATALINA'S *MOLE CARAQUEÑO
de carnero* may have been published in the nineteenth century, but it was probably tested several
centuries earlier in a convent kitchen. And like
any test kitchen, the nuns needed food tasters.

They found their test subjects among the bishops
and friars of the Catholic seminaries, and so, paradoxically, consecrated their gastronomic union in
orgies of sacred music, theater, and poetry.

In sixteenth-, seventeenth-, and eighteenth-
century New Spain, the male religious orders supplied the university and high school professors
who educated the wealthy. The nuns performed
the less glamorous task of educating the daughters of the upper and middle castes. Still, the convent's subordinate role had its benefits. No matter
how rigidly the religious hierarchy cirumscribed
their lives, their roles as teachers gave the nuns
the space to create their own female culture, one
relatively free from the interference of a male-
dominated secular society. Within the convent,
however, the sisters had to comply with a rigid,
authoritarian church dogma paralyzed by Inqui-
sitional paranoia.

60

The Archbishop's Menu

In 1801, the Most Excellent Archbishop of Guadalajara, Juan Cruz Ruiz de Cabañas, established the following menu for the members of the Jesuit seminary:

"The seminarists shall breakfast," he begins, "with a mug of frothy chocolate of regular quality and a prudent ration of bread...and to comply with our nation's ancient custom, *champurrado* [chocolate-flavored corn gruel] may be served to whoever fancies it. Lunch shall commence with a generous and well-seasoned kettle of soup, which may be cooked with lamb, garbanzo, vegetables, or ham, thence to be followed by a light stew or roast, and conclude with a dessert of fresh fruit. For supper everyone shall be served a plate of cooked salad, and mole and beans, and bread, which shall be provided without ration, and if someone shall prefer tortillas... they shall not be denied. In the afternoon at five o'clock bread and fruit shall be ministered to whomever requests it."

Despite their vows of abstinence and poverty, the diet established by the Archbishop for the seminarians was hardly austere. Four daily meals were served in the seminary, compared to five or six served at the tables of Guadalajara's wealthiest families. The upper classes commenced their first meal with the *desayuno*, or breakfast. It was taken at 6 A.M. and consisted of hot chocolate laced with cinnamon, vanilla bean, and ground almond, and accompanied by some bread or pastry. A cup of coffee redolent with cinnamon and raw sugar also was customary. Those with leisure and means enjoyed the *almuerzo*, a brunchlike meal served at about 10 A.M. A nineteenth-century *almuerzo* might consist of a plate of roast shoulder of lamb or pork accompanied by a neatly molded mound of *morisqueta* (white rice wrapped in corn husks and cooked in the soup pot), a plate of refried beans, and frothy tumbler of *pulque* (fermented agave wine) spiked with finely diced onion and chile, or fruits like guava or papaya. If this meal was optional, the next one was not. The *comida*, served at noon, was the day's biggest meal. The *merienda* followed after a few hours of siesta and a few more hours of work. Served at 6 P.M., it consisted of more hot chocolate and something light, perhaps some pasta or tortilla-based recipe, such as a plate of enchiladas. For those who had adopted the European custom of dining, the eating day ended after sunset with the *cena*, or formal dinner. But most, including the cloistered communities, viewed the *cena*, which was served as late as 10 P.M., as another excuse to snack on some *tamales de elote* (sweet fresh corn tamales), a sweet egg bread called a *picón*, and, yes, another mug of chocolate.

The exceptional story of Sor Juana Ines de la Cruz, perhaps the best female poet of the Western hemisphere and early precursor of modern feminism, illustrates the risks of inordinate intellectual brilliance, curiosity, and independence. In her last letter before being forced to renounce the pen, the poet defends the ability of women to think for themselves by slyly comparing her kitchen to the scientific laboratory. But Sor Juana's wit only got her into more trouble. Octavio Paz, in his biography of the Mexican nun, shows how Sor Juana was persecuted into silence for asserting that women should have the right to study and choose careers, and for having the audacity to suggest that God might be female. Still, despite the suffocating conformity the church demanded, the nuns retained a degree of expressive freedom, especially in the arts, which allowed them to nurture their female culture within the cloister.

The nuns, assisted by Indian, *mestiza*, and African servants, excelled at instructing their female students in dance, art, theater, and literature, as well as the so-called domestic arts of sewing, embroidery, cooking, and candy making. In specially designed salons, Paz writes, their young charges performed extravaganzas, while their guests, separated from the players by a handrail, enjoyed exquisite meals and confections prepared by nuns and their students. Not surprisingly, the salons of the convents attracted a devoted following of clerics and nobility. In his fascinating portrait of the salons of Mexico's seventeenth-century convents, the Anglo-American traveler and spy, Thomas Gage, writes:

It is ordinary for the Friars to visit their devoted nuns, and to spend whole days with them, hearing music, feeding on their sweet meats. And for this purpose they have many chambers...with wooden bars between the nuns and them, and in these chambers are tables for the Friars to dine at; and while they dine the nuns recreate them with their voices.

EVEN BISHOPS AND ARCHBISHOPS HAD THEIR favorite nuns, upon whom they counted for songs and for such edible delicacies as Lenten Soup with Shrimp Fritters, Chicken with Fruit in a Red Chile Sauce, or the Almond and Sweet Potatoe Pudding known as "The Clergy's Favorite. Unfortunately, the chroniclers of New Spain did not visit the convent to write about their kitchens. Hence, New Spain did not produce a Brillat-Savarin who could detail their goings-on. The resulting documentary void magnifies the importance of the convent cookbooks, since they provide one of the few direct means of viewing the creation of an emerging *mestizo* cuisine. But as rare books go, they have proved even rarer than the nineteenth-century cookbooks published by Mexico's commercial press. That's why I was surprised to find a convent cookbook, *Collection of Cuisine and Desserts, of the Use and Ownership of the Convent of Religious Ladies of Our Holy Mother of the Immaculate Conception, Year of 1839*, inside the New York City Public Library. The catalogue description merely says that the manuscript was "compiled for use in the kitchen of a Mexican convent."

The recipes offer a wealth of detail about convent cookery, especially when contrasted with

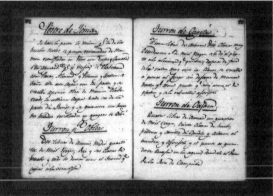

the Spanish cookbooks available at that time. Like Sor Juana's poetry, the convent cooks surpassed the Spanish baroque cuisine. By whatever standard one uses—the number, quantities, or novelty of ingredients, cooking technique, or sheer inventiveness—the convent cookbooks made even the king's recipes look plain by comparison. Convent cooking indulged an opulence of courses, creams, almonds, sugar, eggs, as well as an overabundance of beef, pork, and lamb fed on fields left fallow by decimated indigenous populations. The excesses and inventiveness of convent cooking reflected Mexico's diverse flora and fauna, the omnivorous appetites of its inhabitants, and, above all, the power and wealth of its religious orders.

Rich with tithes, vast ranching and agricultural estates, and culinary and vinting industries, the convent cooks had the wherewithal to create whole new families of recipes. The startling combinations so admired by the baroque aesthetic fostered an openness to New World flavors as well as gluttony. Thus nuns with adventuresome tastes could cook up a different sauce for every day, and not repeat a recipe in a year.

This love of invention also expressed itself in conventional recipes such as the *estofados*, or hearty stews, so essential to Spanish cooking. The only difference between traditional Spanish preparation and the *mestizo* method is that, where a Spanish stew of the late eighteenth century asks for a dozen ingredients, the Mexican nuns routinely tossed in eighteen or twenty.

PAGES FROM THE *Collection of Cuisine and Desserts, of the Use and Ownership of the Convent of Religious Ladies of Our Holy Mother of the Immaculate Conception, Year of 1859.*

The culinary experimentation that served the convents so well suffered several setbacks after Mexico declared its independence from Spain. With varying degrees of success, a chaotic succession of civilian governments, from 1821 to 1877, attacked the excessive privileges, property, and authority of the church bureaucracies. Gradually, as its power was curtailed, the church boarded up convents and seminaries. But these setbacks failed to force the church to give up all of its holdings, nor did they prevent it from continuing its educational mission. Guadalajara illustrates one of its more successful responses to adversity. By means of secret agreements it signed with loyal parishioners, the church maintained control of its convents and seminaries by disguising them as private property. The church further evaded convent and seminary closures by opening new parochial schools and training an army of civilian teachers to do the job once performed by the clergy. In 1876, by order of Archbishop Pedro Loza y Pardavé, eighteen new parochial schools were established, including one in San Pedro Tlaquepaque, the wealthy Guadalajara suburb where Catalina was to begin her teaching career.

Eventually Catalina was promoted to headmistress of the girl's parochial school uptown on Liceo Street, where she administered the education of as many as 120 students between the ages of seven and fifteen. As was typical of parochial and girls' public schools throughout Mexico, Catalina taught a curriculum modeled upon those established by the conventual orders. In addition to reading, writing, and arithmetic, the girls' parochial schools continued to stress Catholic doctrine, art, music, embroidery, sewing, artificial flower making, candy making, and some cooking. These schools not only inspired loyalty to the church; they also trained the daughters of an incipient middle class how to raise children, run households, and manage both servants and husbands. Catalina's cookbook illustrates this aspect of parochial education. She recorded her recipes in a notebook that shares its back pages with lesson plans titled "Problems in Arithmetic," clear evidence that her recipes were used as instructional materials, and thus continuing a tradition of female knowledge started in the convents centuries earlier.

APERETIVO

Otros Chiles en Frío

Chiles Stuffed with Mincemeat with an
Almond-Caper Dressing

Poblano chiles give the best results for this
recipe. The stuffed chiles can be served cold as
an appetizer, or warm as a main dish. The
meatier, triangular-shaped chile's mild bitterness is perfectly suited to the sweet mincemeat.
But Anaheim or New Mexico green chiles are
good substitutes. For tips on how to roast
chiles, see Appendix.

¼ cup whole, blanched, and peeled almonds
2 cups water
¼ cup raisins
2 tablespoons olive oil
2 garlic cloves, minced fine
1 tablespoon finely chopped white onion
½ pound ground lean pork tenderloin
½ pound ground sirloin
1 cup roasted, peeled and pureed tomatoes
¼ teaspoon ground cloves
1 teaspoon salt
⅓ cup finely chopped candied citron (widely
    available ingredient, used in fruitcakes)
½ teaspoon raw or brown sugar
¼ teaspoon ground white pepper
12 large poblano chiles, roasted, sweated,
    and peeled

PREPARATION

Simmer the almonds in 2 cups water for
2 minutes in a 1-quart saucepan. Drain
and cool. Remove the peels by gently rubbing
the almonds between your fingers.

Coarsely chop almonds and raisins
in a food processor and set aside. Heat the oil
in a 12-inch skillet over a medium flame.
Sauté the garlic and onions until the onions
become translucent. Add the ground pork
and beef and continue sautéeing until the meat
mixture is well cooked. Add the pureed
tomato and cloves and sauté 1 minute or so.
Add the remaining ingredients, including
the ground almonds and raisins. Continue
cooking until all the moisture has been
reduced. Set the mincemeat aside to cool.
Spoon each chile with 2 tablespoons of mincemeat stuffing. Arrange the chiles on a bed
of lettuce either on individual plates or a
large platter. Set aside.

CONTINUED ON NEXT PAGE

ALMOND-CAPER DRESSING

1 cup whole almonds
2 tablespoons nonpareil capers
¾ cup virgin olive oil
⅓ cup white wine or pineapple vinager
1 teaspoon salt

Blanch and peel the almonds and place them with the capers in a food processor and grind to a fine paste. Slowly add oil and grind until mixture attains a pesto-like consistency. Pour into a mixing bowl and briskly stir in the vinegar and salt. Spoon dressing over the chiles, making sure that each one is thoroughly covered. SERVES 6 TO 12

SOPA CALDOSA

Sopa de Camarón para Vigilia
Lenten Soup with Shrimp Fritters

This is one of several soups Catalina prepared during Lent, but you don't have to wait until Lent to serve it.

SOUP STOCK

5 cups water
1 yellow onion, quartered
1 bay leaf
½ teaspoon salt
1-½ pounds large, unshelled shrimp

In a large pot, add water, onion, bay leaf, salt, and shrimp. Bring to a boil, cover, and simmer for 5 minutes. Remove shrimp, cool, and peel; set aside enough peeled shrimp to make 1-½ cups of minced shrimp for the shrimp fritters. Reserve the remaining whole shrimp for the soup. Strain shrimp stock, and set aside.

SHRIMP FRITTERS

1 cup *jocoque* (Mexican sour cream),
    or crème fraîche
1 cup finely grated Mexican *cotija* cheese
1-½ cups finely minced boiled shrimp
½ cup sifted flour
1 cup peanut oil

PREPARATION

In a large bowl, thoroughly mix *jocoque*, *cotija* cheese, minced shrimp, and flour. Place the fritter mixture in a pastry tube with a wide tip, and set aside. Heat the peanut oil in a deep, nonstick skillet over a high flame. Press out and cut 1"x 1" fritters and deep fry a few at a time until golden. Remove and drain fritters on paper towels. Keep in a warm oven until serving time.

SOUP

2 medium tomatoes, roasted and peeled
1 medium onion, roasted and peeled
2 tablespoons olive oil
½ teaspoon freshly ground nutmeg
1 bay leaf
½ teaspoon salt
½ teaspoon white pepper
Boiled whole shrimp from stock
5 cups shrimp stock
1 teaspoon finely chopped Italian parsley
⅛ cup very dry sherry

PREPARATION

Over one gas burner, fire-roast the tomatoes directly over the flame. Braise the onion in a dry skillet at a low heat for about 5 minutes. (If you own an electric range, braise both the tomato and onion in a dry iron skillet.) Peel and quarter the tomatoes. Place onion and tomatoes in a blender or food processor and chop to a medium texture; set aside.

Heat the olive oil in a large skillet over a medium flame. Add tomato-onion puree and sauté for 4 minutes over a medium flame. Add nutmeg, bay leaf, salt, and pepper; simmer 1 minute longer. Add remaining whole shrimp and shrimp stock, cover, and simmer for 10 minutes. Pour the soup into a large tureen. Add the shrimp fritters, parsley, and sherry to the broth. Serve immediately.

SERVES 4 TO 5

SOPA SECA

Sopa de Jocoque
Steamed Cream Enchiladas

Not a soup at all, but more like cheese-filled crêpes smothered in a creamy green-chile sauce, this recipe's success depends upon two ingredients: A fresh, unprocessed type of hoop cheese called *panela*; and *jocoque*, a thick but pourable cream that is only slightly soured. Fortunately, several companies distribute both products nationwide. Crème fraîche is a good *jocoque* substitute, conventional sour cream is not; it's just too sour and clumpy.

5 cups water
1 pound *tomatillos*
1 large garlic clove, roasted and peeled
1 teaspoon salt CONTINUED ON NEXT PAGE

5 *cilantro* sprigs

3 green poblano, Anaheim, or New Mexico
   chiles, roasted, peeled, and seeded

1 teaspoon olive oil

3 tablespoons butter

1 dozen corn tortillas

⅔ pound *panela* cheese, cut into long strips

1 cup *jocoque*

3 green poblano, Anaheim, or New Mexico
   chiles, roasted, sweated, peeled, seeded,
   and deveined, sliced into ¼-inch strips
   for garnish

PREPARATION

Bring 5 cups water to a boil in a 3-quart pot,
add the husked *tomatillos*, and parboil for
3 to 4 minutes. Drain the *tomatillos* in a
colander and pour into a food processor.
Blend the *tomatillos* with the garlic, salt,
cilantro sprigs, and 3 chiles for about
20 seconds. Set aside.

In an 8-inch skillet, heat 1 teaspoon of oil
with 2 tablespoons of butter over a low flame,
sautéeing 1 tortilla about 5 seconds on each
side. Gently transfer the tortilla to a 3-quart
Pyrex baking pan attractive enough for table
service, fill it with 2 to 3 strips *panela* cheese,
2 tablespoons *tomatillo* sauce, and then roll it
into an enchilada. Repeat the same procedure
for each enchilada, carefully arranging them
side by side in the pan. Add butter and oil as
needed for sautéeing the remaining tortillas.

Preheat oven to 350 degrees. Pour the
remaining sauce over the rolled enchiladas and
evenly cover them with *jocoque*. Tightly seal the
baking pan with aluminum foil. Pour 2 to 3
cups boiling water inside a bain-marie or double boiler, and gently place the sealed baking
pan in the bain-marie. Bake for 15 minutes.

To serve, lift 2 enchiladas with a spatula
and place them on a plate. Garnish the enchilada with strips of fire-roasted poblano chile.
Serve promptly; this dish does not reheat well.
SERVES 6

PRINCIPIO

Albóndigas Reales

Royal Meatballs

This dish is based on versions found in the
convent cookbook and Trinidad's recipes.
These meatballs are stuffed with sweet
longaniza, almonds, raisins, and olives, and
served with a cinnamon-flavored chile sauce.

MEATBALLS

3 pounds ground boneless pork loin roast

1 egg

2-½ tablespoons finely chopped tomato

¼ large onion, minced

⅓ cup rice, parboiled in 1 cup water
   for 5 minutes, drained and cooled

¼ cup finely chopped Italian parsley
2 tablespoons chopped mint leaves
½ teaspoon salt

STUFFING
½ pound *longaniza* sausage, cooked
    and drained
½ pound ham, minced
⅓ cup pan toasted and coarsely ground
    slivered almonds
⅓ cup raisins
30 stuffed Spanish olives

EGG COATING
3 eggs, slightly beaten
4 ounces plain breadsticks, ground fine
4 tablespoons peanut oil

SAUCE
2 *chile ancho* pods, washed, seeded,
    and deveined
1 tablespoon olive oil
1 cup hot water
1 teaspoon vinegar
1 1-inch cinnamon stick, or 1 teaspoon
    ground cinnamon
3 whole black peppercorns
3 whole cloves
½ teaspoon ground *piloncillo*, or brown sugar
4 tablespoons olive oil
1 cup roasted, peeled, and crushed tomato
2 cups homemade or canned chicken broth

PREPARATION
Mix the ground pork, egg, tomato, onions, rice, parsley, mint, and salt together in a large bowl. Set aside.

Remove the *longaniza* sausage from its casing. Crumble the sausage into a preheated 8-inch skillet, and sauté for 5 minutes. If the *longaniza* lacks fat, add 1 teaspoon of olive oil to prevent it from sticking. Drain all the fat from the pan before adding the ham, almonds, and raisins. Stir these ingredients together, then set aside.

To stuff meatballs, first spoon out 2 table-spoons of the meatball mixture and gently flat-ten with the palm of your hand against a clean surface covered with wax paper until it forms a round, ¼-inch-thick patty. Lift the patty from the wax paper with a spatula, then place a heaping teaspoon of the stuffing mixture and 1 olive in the middle of the patty. Fold the patty over the stuffing and olive, making sure to cover completely. Shape the meatball into a smooth ball by gently rolling it in the palm of your hands; it should measure about 1-½ inches in diameter.

To cook the meatballs, bring 2 quarts water to a rolling boil in a 5-quart kettle. Drop the meatballs one by one into the water. Remove them as they float to the surface, drain in a colander, and cool.

Dip the meatballs in egg batter and roll them in bread crumbs. Heat 4 tablespoons peanut oil in a 10-inch skillet over a medium flame.

CONTINUED ON NEXT PAGE↪

Sauté the meatballs until golden, then drain on a paper towel. This recipe makes about 30 meatballs. Serve them hot with the following sauce:

MEATBALL SAUCE

In a small skillet, sauté the *chile anchos* skins in 1 tablespoon preheated olive oil for 30 seconds. Soak the toasted chile skins in 1 cup hot water and 1 teaspoon vinegar for 2 hours. Place a heavy plate over the chiles to completely submerge them under water. Grind the chile skins in a blender to a smooth paste. Pour into a bowl, and set aside. Rinse blender with a tablespoon of water and save the remaining paste. In a mortar and pestle or a food processor, grind cinnamon, peppercorns, and cloves to a powder, and set aside. Place a *piloncillo* cone inside a plastic sandwich bag and crush with a mallet. Measure ½ teaspoon of the crushed *piloncillo*, and set aside.

Heat 4 tablespoons oil in a 12-inch skillet over a medium flame. Sauté the spices long enough to release their aroma, then pour in the *chile ancho* paste, *piloncillo*, and pureed tomatoes. Simmer the sauce for 2 minutes over a medium flame, stirring constantly to prevent sticking. Add the broth and simmer for another 5 minutes. Place the *albóndigas* in the sauce and simmer another 5 minutes or until they are thoroughly heated. Serve 3 meatballs on a plate and cover with 3 tablespoons of sauce.

SERVES 6 TO 8

Guisado al Ajiaco

Chicken with Fruit in a Red-Chile Sauce

Versions of this dish appear in the convent and published cookbooks, both of which share two ingredients—fruit and *ají*, the word for chile used in the Caribbean and South America. I prefer the recipe we developed from the convent's cookbook. We've found that substituting the chicken with a quince and a large green apple transforms this offering into a vegetarian *ajiaco*.

4 *chiles anchos* washed, seeded, and deveined
1 teaspoon olive oil
½ teaspoon white wine vinegar
⅓ cup dry pan toasted sesame seeds
1-¼ cup soaking solution
3 small zucchini, cut into 1-inch slices
2-½ cups *puchero* (see p. 26) or chicken broth
2 tablespoons butter
1 large ripe plantain, cut into ½-inch
    diagonal slices
3 tablespoons olive oil
2 large garlic cloves, minced fine
1 large bay leaf
1 teaspoon finely chopped Italian parsley
3 large chicken breasts, halved
Salt to taste

PREPARATION

Heat the oil in a medium skillet over a medium flame. Sauté the *ancho* skins for 30 seconds. Soak the toasted chile skins for 2 hours in warm water with ½ teaspoon vinegar. Toast the sesame seeds in a dry pan until brown and set aside (see Appendix). Place the soaked *ancho* skins in a blender with the sesame seeds and 1 cup soaking solution. Grind to a thick, smooth paste. Add ¼ cup soaking solution if needed to remove any paste remaining in the blender. Using a plastic spatula or wooden spoon, pour the chile paste into a bowl, and set aside.

In a medium saucepan, parboil the sliced zucchini for 3 minutes in 1 cup broth. Remove the zucchini, and set aside. Heat 2 tablespoons butter in a large skillet over a medium flame. Sauté the plaintain until lightly browned, and set aside.

In the same skillet, heat 3 tablespoons oil over a medium flame. Sauté the garlic, bay leaf, and parsley for 1 minute. Add the chicken breasts and sauté until lightly browned. Remove breasts, and set aside.

In the same skillet, sauté the *ancho* paste for 3 minutes, stirring steadily to prevent burning or sticking. Add 1-½ cups chicken broth to *ancho* paste. Carefully stir until fully blended. Return chicken breasts, plantains, and zucchini to the sauce. Add salt to taste. Simmer 5 minutes over a low flame.

SERVES 6

ASADO

Carnero Tatemado

Roast Lamb

Use this mildly herbal and piquant gravy with the roast lamb recipe (see Index).

GRAVY

1 teaspoon olive oil
2 *chile ancho* pods, washed, seeded, and deveined
2 cups warm water
1 teaspoon vinegar
2-½ cups lamb or chicken broth (canned is fine)
2 tablespoons olive oil
2 garlic cloves, minced
1-½ tablespoons toasted flour
1 teaspoon salt

Before you begin to roast the lamb prepare the chile sauce. Heat 1 teaspoon olive oil in a medium skillet over a medium flame. Sauté the chile skins for 30 seconds, stirring constantly. Soak the toasted *ancho* skins in a bowl for 2 hours in 2 cups warm water and 1 teaspoon vinegar. Place a heavy plate atop the chiles to submerge them under water. After soaking, place the *ancho* skins in a blender with ½ cup soaking solution and process to a smooth paste. Pour in a bowl, and set aside.

CONTINUED ON NEXT PAGE ⮑

In a deep saucepan over a medium flame, bring the broth to a boil and simmer 10 minutes. Heat 2 tablespoons oil in a 12-inch skillet over a medium flame. Sauté the garlic for 30 seconds. Add the flour and continue sautéeing for 1 minute until it turns golden. Pour the chile paste into the skillet, sauté for 1 minute, stirring constantly, using a whisk to thoroughly blend and prevent burning or sticking. Slowly pour in the lamb broth and 1 teaspoon salt, whisking continually to make a smooth gravy. Pour the sauce into a gravy bowl.

SERVES 6 TO 7

ENSALADA GUISADA

Ensalada de Coliflor

Cauliflower Salad

1 quart water
1-½ teaspoon salt
1 whole cauliflower, cut into florets
¼ cup olive oil
1 tablespoon finely minced garlic
½ white onion, sliced thin
½ teaspoon dried oregano
⅛ cup white wine vinegar
1 large ripe avocado, peeled, seeded, and cut into 1-inch cubes
20 Spanish green olives
7 pickled yellow chiles (*tornachiles*)
4 sprigs Italian parsley

Bring 1 quart water to a boil in a large kettle over a high flame, then reduce to medium. Stir in 1 teaspoon salt, add the cauliflower and simmer for 5 minutes. Pour the cauliflower into a colander while it is still firm and quickly rinse with cold water. Place cauliflower in a large mixing bowl, and set aside. Heat ¼ cup olive oil in a 10-inch skillet over a medium flame. Sauté the garlic until it takes on a light golden color. Add onions and oregano and sauté 1 minute longer. Pour the hot oil mixture over the cauliflower. Add white wine vinegar, avocado, olives, chiles, and the remaining

½ teaspoon salt to the salad. Gently toss. Chill for 2 hours before serving on a platter. Garnish with parsley sprigs. SERVES 5 TO 6

Leche de Camote Morado y Almendra

Almond and Sweet Potato Pudding

This recipe goes by at least two names. Catalina called it *Leche de Camote Morado y Almendra*. We found an exact duplicate of it in the convent cookbook titled *The Clergy's Favorite*. We've dressed it up a bit by topping it with a dash of whipped cream.

4 pounds sweet potatoes, cut into 1-inch slices
2 cups water
8 cups milk
1-½ cups sugar
¾ cup toasted, slivered, and coarsely
    ground almonds
2 tablespoons toasted slivered almonds
½ pint whipping cream, whipped
½ teaspoon cinnamon

PREPARATION

Preheat oven to 300 degrees. To an 8-quart kettle with 2 cups water, add potatoes and steam for 30 to 40 minutes. Remove potato slices without breaking them, drain and cool before peeling. Gently remove skins with your fingers. Mash the potatoes in a large mixing bowl, then strain through a fine sieve. This yields about 6 cups of strained sweet potatoes. Set aside.

To toast the almonds, place them on a cookie sheet in preheated oven for 15 minutes. Shake the cookie sheet once or twice while in the oven. Set aside 2 tablespoons toasted almonds for the topping. Grind the remaining almonds in a food processor, and set aside.

Pour 8 cups milk, 1-½ cups sugar, the ground almonds, and pureed sweet potatoes into a heavy, 8-quart kettle. Stir until blended. Bring mixture to a boil, reduce heat to low, and simmer for 35 minutes, stirring constantly with a wire whisk until mixture thickens. Remove kettle from stove and thoroughly stir in the ground almonds. Pour mixture into a large, shallow dish or individual dessert cups. Decorate each serving with a dollop of whipped cream, a dusting of cinnamon, and some of the toasted slivered almonds. SERVES 6 TO 8

beyond recipes: a woman's world

———————————◆———————————

ATALINA'S CONCERNS REACHED FAR beyond the kitchen. I know this from her poem "The Vertigo" and its preface, which she addressed to a Señor D. J. Martínez Parra:

My dear friend: several times, upon reading my lyrical compositions, you slipped into my life the tempting insinuation that I write a poem which reflects upon the ideas, the sentiments and the struggles of our epoch, as rich in high ideals as in tragic events. Carried away by the affection you profess to me, you exaggerated the ability of my creative powers to attempt such an arduous enterprise, one upon which others have dashed their ingenuity, and which presents all the characteristics of an impossible task.

The poem and preface are undated, yet Catalina's political, philosophical, and literary references suggest that she wrote them some time after the election of Porfirio Díaz to the presidency in 1877. The struggles between the liberals, who fought to defend and modernize the Mexican secular state, and conservatives, who sought to protect the church and its privileges, continued to preoccupy intellectuals of Catalina's generation. We can hear the echo of this ideological war in her poem, which tells of a to-the-death struggle between two brothers who represent different political and philosophical tendencies.

The poem's characters, moralizing tone and would have been familiar to a Mexican reader of her time. The literary model for Catalina's feuding brothers can be found in a popular nineteenth-century play, *Don Juan Tenório*, written by Spanish playwright José Zorrilla. This religious drama published in 1844 tells how a woman's love inspires the play's Don Juan character to repent and save his macho soul. Catalina's poem, however, transforms the relationship between two of Zorrilla's characters.

In Catalina's poem, Don Juan and his fellow libertine and rival, Don Luis, become brothers *and* mortal enemies. Her poem begins with Don Juan returning in rage to the "secular tower" where he has imprisoned his brother. Soon after entering his cell, Don Luis dares his brother to take his life:

> Wound me, if you intend to;
> Serenely I await the blow,
> Since I, in turn, condemn you
> To the torment of living.
> Where shall you escape
> That punishment sha'n't
>   find you?
> In vain, other shores,
> other climes shall shelter you,
> Yet, where ever you go
> your crimes shall follow.

And so, Catalina turns Zorrilla's religious fantasy into a philosophical and political allegory. Clearly, Don Juan represents the radical anticlerical liberals. Don Luis appears to represent the moderate liberals and conservatives allied with Díaz. It may also be that Catalina's Luis represents an actual person, perhaps Luis Curiel, the governor of Jalisco, who instituted reforms that permitted students educated in parochial schools to graduate to public secondary schools and colleges. A teacher like Catalina would have welcomed Curiel's reforms, officially putting the church-run schools on a par with the public schools. But she also would have known how Curiel's reforms had angered the radical liberals, who feared the church's resurgence in the educational arena.

Whatever the symbolism, Catalina's poem expressed her view of history as a metaphysical struggle, a distinctly positivist perspective. The idea that Latin America had reached the threshold of a new phase of social and cultural evolution, one which would usher in a civilization based upon spiritual principles, was fashionable among intellectuals of her generation schooled on French positivist philosophy. They believed the Díaz regime promised to transcend liberal and conservative feuding by using scientific pragmatism to create a modern secular state that preserved the church's role of moral anchor.

City dwellers like Catalina could not or did not wish to see how the Díaz regime's positivist credo of "order and progress" justified ruinous agrarian policies and brutal repression of workers and peasants. Nor did they anticipate the revolt and the economic chaos that later reduced her mother, Trinidad, and her sister to penury. Instead, Catalina hoped that a new society based upon scientific knowledge would replace the previous one, which the liberals had failed to reform by means of laws and constitutions.

That's what is so intriguing about Catalina. She thoroughly contradicted my preconceived notions of the devout Catholic spinster, who, after teaching young women to read, write, and become doting wives, retired to a solitary, uneventful life. Catalina had ideas, and she expressed them with confidence. You hear it when she speaks of her "compositions," and her poem's grand intentions. Here's a person quite at ease with the notion of female authorship. And the point of the preface itself, which lauds freedom of inquiry, not only expresses positivist idealism, but a self-consciousness that could only be called intellectual.

As a director of a girls' Catholic school, Catalina answered to the Archbishop of Guadalajara, one of Mexico's most powerful and conservative prelates. Yet she reserved for herself the right to enjoy freedoms espoused by freethinking liberals. Worse, she privately shared her ideas with Señor Martínez Parra, a man whom my Aunt Estela flatly described as a Free Mason, which put him on the side of radical liberals, who were habitually at war with the local church hierarchy—another heresy.

Catalina had been courted by Señor Parra, but his political loyalties made it impossible for her to accept his hand in marriage. Catalina would have been summarily dismissed from her job were she to accept Martínez's proposal. The archbishop would never permit such an outrage. Her actions were thus motivated by fear of reprisal, pressure to conform to the political etiquette of her day, and something more.

Obviously, Catalina could have followed the example of her sisters by marrying and bearing children. That would have been the easy choice. But I suspect that Catalina declined Señor Parra's proposal because she valued her right to a career more than marriage. With her modest profession she freed herself from grinding domesticity and

fulfilled her obligation to her widowed mother, who would later depend upon her daughter for support. Yet, in choosing the spinster's life, she accepted certain risks. Like other women of her day, she would have had an acute sense of limits, a double awareness with which she weighed her actions: a desire to satisfy her deepest personal needs, and the vigilance to protect herself from disapproving gossip. She would have heard the chorus of male voices in the Mexican press who warned against allowing women to school themselves, launch careers, rent apartments, and, worst of all, remain unmarried. Catalina did all these things, which exposed her to the ire of conservative and liberal male writers alike. These writers denigrated the spinster as an emasculated women of lesbian inclinations who threatened the sanctity of married life.

Censure of this sort must have inspired caution, if not fear. I can see her, pausing late in the day, unseen in an empty classroom, her hand resting chalk point against slate at midrecipe, the one her class would copy the next day, reflecting upon her prudent independence. Despite our decade's obsession with biography, no amount of private detail can completely dissolve the distances that separate us. Yet I do know enough about Catalina to compare her to Mexican women of her Victorian generation.

Historian Silvia Marina Arrom, in *The Women of Mexico: 1790 to 1857*, writes that the image of nineteenth-century Mexican women as "ignorant and idle women, living in rigid enclosure" was a revisionist exaggeration proffered by Mexican liberals trying to invalidate the Spanish colonial order they had overthrown. Early accounts of travel by writers such as Fanny Calderón de la Barca, the Scottish wife of Spain's first minister to independent Mexico, also contributed to the image of Mexican women as the servile possessions of brutish husbands, a view later recanted by Fanny herself.

Catalina actually represented a new, yet little-recognized elite of nineteenth-century Latin American women who acquired educations and launched careers. Admittedly, their numbers were small and usually restricted to the *mestizas* from

CATALINA AT AGE 16.

the lower and middle class in the largest cities. Still, the social and political impact of allowing women to educate themselves and choose careers in low status professions represented a significant advance over the previous century. The change came gradually. Late in the eighteenth century, government ministers in Madrid enacted reforms designed to stimulate Spain's lagging productive capacity by integrating women into the national economy. These reforms were later transplanted to New Spain.

The most dramatic of these reforms altered the legal status of Mexican women, particularly for the women of the middle and lower classes, since they had the most to gain from education and steady employment. In January, 1799, the Spanish government abolished laws that permitted Mexico's male-only guilds to bar women from engaging in manufacturing activities. In 1786, Spanish officials ordered the convents to open girls' public primary schools in Mexico City. Seventeen years later, in 1803, the convents were ordered to open girls' public schools throughout New Spain, including several in Guadalajara. These reforms were motivated by political and economic considerations, not liberal egalitarianism. The government reasoned that educated women would raise better educated, more productive sons, as well as administer healthier, more efficient households. Just as importantly, educating women of the lower classes promised to create a new reserve of surplus labor.

After independence from Spain in 1821, Mexican *criollas* and *mestizas* who had benefited from earlier reforms slowly relinquished political responsibilities earned during the insurrection. The wartime competence they demonstrated as spies, gunrunners, lobbyists, and fund-raisers encouraged the leaders of the new republic to continue the process of educational reform. In 1842, the Mexican government passed laws mandating the education of girls and boys between the ages of seven and fifteen. The Mexican government abolished the guild system fifteen years later. Twelve years after that, the government followed through on its promise to establish the nation's first women's public secondary school. This slow pace of educational reforms had, by midcentury, increased the ranks of female teachers, an achievement, Arrom writes, that paid crucial dividends:

> Not only did their job opportunities expand as the demand for girls' schools grew, but the occupation of schoolmistress gained prestige as more qualified teachers taught older students at a higher level than before. Teachers showed a growing professionalism and even a sense of mission as the century progressed.

Neither the Spanish nor the Mexican reforms were intended to increase female authority in public life. Nevertheless, liberal educational reforms had the unintended effect of helping the Catholic church recoup powers it lost after independence. So, even as convents were boarded up, The Company of Mary opened dozens of public schools for girls, and educated a generation of teachers for the new parochial schools.

After Mexico City, Guadalajara became the nation's second-most important arena for educational reform. Early in the century, the city had already witnessed a steady increase in the number of primary public and parochial schools for boys and girls. By the 1870s the pace of reform quickened there when federal and state governments seized upon public schooling as a means of molding a middle class that could rally to the defense of the civil state. The liberals believed that these new secular loyalties could not be forged without also diminishing the church's power over everyday citizens. And what better arena to battle for the city's hearts and minds than in the new public schools? Archbishop Pedro Loza y Pardavé responded to this threat by pushing for the creation of new parochial schools to resume the religious and political indoctrination once dominated by the convents. Except that now, the parochial schools aggressively educated the children of the same incipient middle class the public schools hoped to enroll. Women, both as teachers and as students, profited from this competition. Expanding parochial and public educational opportunities for girls during the 1870s and 1880s boosted the demand for female teachers like Catalina. By century's end, the number of women's high schools, teacher training colleges, and trade schools firmly established education as an avenue for female professional advancement in the largest cities. Still, Archbishop Pardavé's mission to politicize parochial schooling did not reduce teachers like Catalina to mindless pawns, as the liberal politicos accused. If anyone knew this, it was the man for whom Catalina wrote her poems, Señor Martínez Parra.

CLASS PICTURE
A COPY OF WHICH WAS SENT TO CATALINA BY HER SISTER, MARIA,
ON HER SAINT'S DAY, SEPTEMBER 7, 1907.
CATALINA IS THE TALLEST WOMAN,
THIRD FROM THE LEFT, IN THE BACK ROW.

In her preface, she sounds quite the positivist, when she argued that history was driven by the forces of a metaphysical dialectic:

> The antinomies and rebellions which always engender the march of ideas...are the most powerful stimulus for human progress, for the day in which contradiction is extinguished, if this were possible, intelligence would become as still as the blood of a corpse.

Elsewhere, she exalts the nobility of unrestricted inquiry by personifying it as a spirit which,

> . . . pushed onward by the insatiable demon of investigation, soars to the exalted heights and descends to the deepest abyss, climbs the skies and submerges itself in the world's muddy quagmires so that it may see it, feel it, and know it all.

Her near-carnal language contrasts with the morbidly fatalistic catechisms she, as headmistress, required her teachers to impart. The contrast between her day job, as it were, and her private thoughts reveals a modern self as fragmented as our own; only the competing loyalties differ. Catalina built walls to keep her two worlds apart. She knew her superiors would frown upon her private musings because of her freethinking sympathies, and because she expressed her ideas with passionate abandon to a man, a display of intimacy not permissible in public.

It is doubtful that Catalina would have traded her independence, as restricted and conflicted as it was, for the certainties of marriage. She instead chose a career, even if its objective was to train housewives—a vocation she'd rejected for herself. She could reconcile this contradiction by remembering the past. She knew Mexico's nineteenth-century middle-class woman ruled domains worth defending. Something as seemingly mundane as the teaching of recipes could be appreciated for bolstering the influence of women at home and in the classroom—two spheres within which Catalina had earned a measure of equality. Fortunately, my grandmother, Delfina, was sent to Catalina's school. In the sanctuary of her classroom, Catalina, the schoolmarm, offered Delfina a taste of independence, an example that my grandmother took further than her aunt could have dared.

CHAPTER EIGHT

a day in the country

EXCEPT FOR THE WEALTHY, WHO COULD afford to spend a year in Paris, a vacation for a family of Catalina's class consisted of a visit with their relatives in the countryside, or a few days' stay at a resort hotel on the shores of Lake Chapala, Mexico's largest freshwater lake about thirty miles southwest of Guadalajara.

Catalina, I learned, did visit the countryside and taste its cuisine. But I have no evidence of her going on holiday to Chapala, though she would have had plenty of opportunities. She could have made the day's journey by stagecoach, mule-drawn trolley, rail, or a combination of these conveyances. Or she simply could have waited for Chapala's fish and its recipes to arrive in Guadalajara's marketplaces.

Prior to the extension of rail service to the lake, some fish, like the *pescado blanco*, a delicately flavored, white-fleshed species native to Chapala, were placed, while still alive, in water-filled barrels, which were then carried by mules into the city. Whitefish, catfish, bass, in addition to minnows called *charales* were also dried at the lake's shore and sold in Guadalajara. Lake Chapala has since fallen on hard times. The unquenchable thirsts of Mexico City and Guadalajara, relentless irrigation, and modern factories along the shore have depleted the lake's abundant wildlife. But Ana Ugarte, who was born at the turn of the century to an illustrious landowning family, still remembers Chapala's former generosity: "At the village of Chacaltita, on Saturday afternoons, the shores became crowded with canoes that came in from all around the lake loaded with goods." Fish, frogs, crayfish, even ducks and water birds netted in the lake squirmed in canoe hulls next to mounds of tomatoes, corn, and multicolored chiles. But Ana's parents searched for something special on market days —the prized *pescado blanco*. After shopping, her family retired to her aunt's lakeside home for lunch. Usually, the fish was fried in an egg white batter and served with a salsa made with *chile cascabel*, or rattle chile, named for the sound its seeds make when dried. But *pescado blanco*, Ana recalls, could be served up fancy, too. Typically, the fish was stuffed with a tomato, parsley, and roasted green chile sauce, then wrapped in parchment paper, and deep fried or placed over a grill, *en pabillote*-style. Obviously, these parchment-wrapped recipes betray a French influence.

But nothing in Mexican cuisine is ever so simple. The Purepecha, or Tarascan civilization that rivaled the Aztecs and colonized Chapala long before the Spaniards arrived, also loved to stuff and wrap their fish in corn husks and other flavorful leaves. So, as with so many *mestizo* recipes, we find a confluence of traditions. The French style of cooking with parchment paper replaced corn husks while Spanish ingredients such as olives and capers were incorporated into local stuffing recipes designed for the fish native to Chapala and the lakes of the neighboring state of Michoacan.

REGARDLESS OF WHETHER CATALINA VISITED Chapala, she surely visited her relatives in the countryside more than once. The first time was early in 1894, when a young man named José

Velasco asked for the hand of Catalina's younger sister, Juanita.

The romance began sometime after José had joined a Guadalajara seminary. At first, becoming a priest seemed more appealing than farming. But José suffered a lapse of faith after meeting Juanita, and quit the seminary. After months of closely watched visits, José invited Juanita's family, including Catalina, to *La Sauceda*, the hacienda purchased by José's grandfather in the early nineteenth century.

The journey began by train, ended by carriage or stagecoach, and required the better part of a day to complete. During their visit, the Vargas family would have been treated to the obligatory picnic. Imagine a grand procession of uncles, aunts, and cousins, some on horseback, others loaded in wagons with the day's victuals packed in wicker baskets. The delicacies served that day reflected the intimate ties binding city folk to their

country relatives. Juanita, no doubt, used some of the recipes she'd learned in her mother's kitchen in Guadalajara; perhaps her recipe for *chiles poblanos* stuffed with sardines marinated in a Dijon dressing to show off her city-bred tastes. The cold meat dishes called *fiambres*, the quichelike *tortes* of string beans and fresh cheeses made by José's mother, and the long, spindled ears of white corn picked from a nearby field and roasted in a fire made from dried cornstalks, represented the hacienda's contribution to the meal.

The hacienda that Catalina had visited had already seen better days. For the first three hundred years of Mexico's history, the huge grain and ranching estates of Jalisco grew rich provisioning the mining enterprises in western Mexico. These haciendas, which resembled small company towns, employed scores of servants, tradesmen, and peasants in tanneries, grain mills, distilleries, sugar mills, soap factories, mining operations, as well as in ranching and farming. Some haciendas built their own chapels and schools. Other *ranchero* families hired tutors and sent their sons to universities in Guadalajara, Mexico City, or Paris. Juanita's son, Julio, remembers that the *casco*, or administrative compound, of his grandfather's hacienda had its own library. But as the hacienda system waned in the late eighteenth century, the descendants of the region's first European colonists sold off chunks of their haciendas to a new generation of *rancheros* like José's father, Teófilo, who bought a portion of a preexisting estate near the town of Zapotlanejo, a place named by the Indians for its zapote groves. José would later inherit the least

productive share of the estate when his father died. His brothers decided that José deserved no better since he spent his time at the *jalipéos* (rodeos) playing the *charro* (or skilled horseman).

José grumbled but accepted his lot. He and Juanita did the best they could with their share of land, which wasn't enough. So José moved his family to Zapotlanejo, and worked as an *administrador de hacienda*, or overseer to an estate. The work, when he had it, paid well. At that time, men with knowledge of both bookkeeping and farming were well rewarded for seeing to it that the landlord's hacienda turned a profit raising cash crops for export. So, for a time, José provided his family a degree of comfort, even if all around them the peasants grew hungrier as the haciendas produced less and less for local marketplaces.

But the revolution of 1910, and its recurring political and economic crises, made life both bleak and dangerous. More than once José found himself up to his neck in mossy water, looking up from the bottom of a hacienda's well, as he hid from marauding revolutionaries and bandits. Naturally, since the landlords had retreated to Guadalajara, the revolutionaries saw overseers like José as stand-ins for the wealthy they longed to punish. It wasn't long before José saw the foolishness of risking his life for another man's land. In 1923, José and his sons joined the rail gangs building the Southern Pacific link between Magdalena, Jalisco and Tepic, Nayarit. The steep, treacherous canyons separating northern Jalisco from the mountains of Nayarit to the north made progress slow and dangerous. A year later, José, his pockets weighted with gold coins, gathered up Juanita and the kids, and rode the Southern Pacific line north to Mexicali. José and Juanita crossed the border, entering Calexico on April 14, 1924. Sometime after, they settled in Los Angeles, and so established a way station for relatives who would follow, including my grandmother Delfina and her recipes.

CATALINA VISITED *LA SAUCEDA* SEVERAL TIMES. One occasion was the marriage of Julio's eldest brother, *also* named José, in June 1912, the first of several marriages uniting the descendants of Catalina's family with the Velascos.

Julio recounted his brother's wedding feast: "José looked like one of those guys in a *charro* movie," Julio said of his handsome figure on horseback, silver buckles gleaming on his tight-fitting riding outfit. "They married in Juanacatlan and rode to my Uncle Pancho's ranch on horseback, . . . bridesmaids, wedding party and all. They even had a mariachi with a big bass drum, and from far away you could hear them ride toward the ranch. 'Here they come. Here come the newlyweds,'" he remembers yelling in astonishment.

Waiting in the compound of his uncle's ranch were large bowl-shaped pots of red and green moles, and refried beans spiced with *chorizo* and toasted ground chile seeds, all kept warm on wood fires. And there, next to the fire pits, was *"la molienda,"* a corps of kneeling women grinding corn washerwoman style on big metates. Their job was to grind enough *nixtamal*, or lime-cooked corn dough, to warm the hand of every guest with a tortilla hot off the *comal*. Catalina was there for the wedding, and the visits that led up to it. Tortilla in hand, one can imagine Catalina chatting with fellow wedding guests, perhaps discussing politics, poetry, or the edible delights of the previous day's picnic under the willow trees, while pausing to commit to memory the tastes she savored at the wedding feast.

Elotes Tatemados

Field Roasted Corn

When corn is roasted whole and unshucked, the green husks not only seal in heat, they steam into each ear a delicate, smoky sweetness perfectly accented with a pinch of salt, a squeeze of lime, and a dusting of lip-stinging chile. There are no strict measurements or roasting times for this recipe. It is all a matter of taste and timing.

10 dry *chiles pequínes*
1 dozen ears unhusked sweet corn,
    yellow or white
1 dozen Mexican limes, halved
5 teaspoons salt dissolved in 1 cup water
¼ cup butter or margarine, melted,
    or ¼ cup mayonnaise

In a large, heavy, dry skillet over a medium flame, sauté chiles for about 30 seconds or until they turn a dark red. Using a blender or food processor, finely grind the *chiles pequínes*, and set aside.

Place the unhusked ears on the barbecue and roast for 30 minutes. Remove the ears, cool, take off the outer leaves and silk, and return them to the barbecue. Brush each ear with a coat of salt water, then a heavy coat of butter, margarine, or mayonnaise.

Roast the ears over the coals until the kernels have turned a golden color and the marinade has soaked into each ear. Squeeze lime juice on the ears and dust with a pinch of toasted ground chile. Sprinkle with salt to taste.
SERVES 12

Chiles en Mostaza

Green Chiles in a Dijon Sauce

Quality sardines are essential to this recipe. We recommend Spanish sardines packed in lemon or orange wedges and olive oil because their dressings won't clash with the vinaigrette. Spanish sardines are also firmer than other brands, which makes them easier to stuff inside the chiles.

CHILES
1 dozen poblano, Anaheim, or green
    New Mexico chiles, roasted, sweated,
    and peeled
4 cans (125 grams each) Spanish sardines
    in olive oil, drained

CONTINUED ON NEXT PAGE⮠

DRESSING

4 tablespoons white wine vinegar
4 tablespoons Dijon mustard
1 teaspoon salt
1 teaspoon white pepper
⅔ cup olive oil

GARNISH

2 teaspoons capers
8 large green olives
6 yellow pickled chiles, or 6 pickled serrano
    chiles
4 sprigs Italian parsley
½ white onion, sliced into thin rings
½ romaine or butter lettuce, rinsed
    and drained, cut into salad-size pieces

Cut a 2-inch slit down from the stem end
of each roasted and peeled chile. Carefully
remove seeds without damaging the chile.
Stuff the chiles with 1 or 2 sardines, and
set aside.

   Make a traditional Dijon dressing by first
blending vinegar, mustard, salt, and pepper
in a large stainless-steel mixing bowl. Then
slowly drizzle olive oil into the bowl while
steadily beating the dressing with a wire
whisk. Take your time. You want to incorpo-
rate air into the mixture to give it a fine,
frothy texture.

Serving options:

1) On a serving platter covered with lettuce,
arrange the chiles in a geometric design, and
pour on the Dijon vinaigrette. Garnish with
capers, olives, pickled yellow or serrano chiles,
and a few sprigs of Italian parsley.

2) Make lettuce salads on individual plates.
Top each salad with 1 or 2 stuffed chiles and
dress with onion rings and Dijon vinaigrette.

SERVES 6 TO 12

Torta de Ejotes

String Bean Torte

Although this recipe is called a torte, it is more like a layered quiche, so you can enjoy it warm or cold for breakfast, lunch, or on a Sunday picnic.

3 cups string beans, cut into 3-inch pieces
½ quart water
3 tablespoons olive oil
1-½ cups tomato, diced
½ medium white onion, sliced into thin rings
½ teaspoon salt
¼ cup butter
10 extra-large eggs, beaten
1 cup thinly sliced *panela* cheese or
    mozzarella cheese
½ cup grated *cotija* cheese or Romano cheese
6 *cilantro* sprigs

Preheat oven to 350 degrees. Parboil the string beans in a medium saucepan filled with ½ quart water for 5 minutes. Remove the beans and drain. Heat the oil in a 12-inch, ovenproof skillet over a medium flame. Sauté the tomato, onions, and string beans over a medium flame for 5 minutes. Stir in ½ teaspoon salt, remove the vegetables without pouring out any oil, and cool. Slowly melt ¼ cup butter in the same skillet and heat over a medium flame. Coat the bottom of the skillet with 1 cup beateneggs and allow them to thicken slightly before covering with ½ cup of *panela* cheese.

Reduce heat to low and layer with half of the sautéed string beans, tomatoes, and onions. Add ½ cup layer of *panela* cheese and cover with the remaining string beans, tomato, and onions. Layer the torte with the remaining beaten eggs. Top with grated *cotija* cheese. Place ovenproof skillet in the oven for 20 minutes. Test the torte with a toothpick to make sure it's thoroughly cooked. Garnish with *cilantro* sprigs. SERVES 6 OR 7

Otro Lomo Frío

Another Cold Roast Beef

The first Spaniards to settle in New Spain didn't take to native foods right away. Instead, they followed their stomachs to the temperate highland plateaus, where they revived Old World diets based on the cultivation of wheat, oats, barley, garbanzos, and wine grapes, as well as cattle and sheep grazing. The *lomo* or shoulder roast recipes symbolizes this history. The hacienda cooks turned to the *fiambres* to preserve the big beef cuts best suited for roasting.

3 pounds London broil roast, at least
    1-½ inches thick and butterflied

MARINADE

3 garlic cloves, minced
4 whole cloves
12 whole black peppercorns
3 tablespoons white wine
1 tablespoon finely grated fresh ginger
½ teaspoon salt

STUFFING

¾ cup crumbled *longaniza* sausage, cooked
    and drained
1 teaspoon olive oil (optional)
3 serrano chiles, seeded and minced
¾ cup finely ground ham

BASTING

1 tablespoon red wine vinegar
1 tablespoon fresh chopped oregano or 1
    teaspoon dry oregano
½ teaspoon fresh thyme or ¼ teaspoon
    dry thyme
½ teaspoon salt

GARNISH

3 pickled yellow chiles, seeded and minced
1 bunch radishes, cut into rosettes
½ head lettuce
1 ripe avocado, peeled and sliced
½ cup whole green olives
24 inches string for tying the roast

To Butterfly the Roast:

Lay the roast on a heavy-duty cutting board, then slice the meat lengthwise at ½-inch of thickness, carefully lifting back the upper half of the roast as if opening a book. Stop cutting 2 inches short of slicing the roast completely in two. The roast should double in width. Hammer it steadily with the flat part of a meat mallet until it is ½-inch thick.

Finely grind garlic, cloves, and peppercorns in a food processor or blender. Place in a small bowl and add wine, grated ginger, and salt. Rub the meat on both sides with the marinade and place it in the refrigerator for 3 hours.

Remove the *longaniza* sausage from its casing and gently crumble into a preheated, 10-inch skillet. Add 1 teaspoon olive oil if the sausage begins to stick. Add the minced chiles, and sauté over a low flame for 2 minutes. Drain the fat rendered from the *longaniza*. Place the sausage in a large bowl, add the ham, and mix well. Set aside.

Place the London broil on a large roasting pan, spread the stuffing over the meat, then firmly roll the meat up starting from the longest side. Remove excess stuffing. Cut about 2 feet of cooking string, tie the meat roll off at one end, leaving enough string to tightly coil up the rolled meat with half-hitches spaced about 2 inches apart. Rub the roast with the basting mixture of vinegar, oregano, thyme, and salt. Preheat oven to 350 degrees.

Heat 2 tablespoons of olive oil in a 12-inch skillet over a medium flame and braise the roast on all sides until browned. Place the roll in a large roasting pan and roast in oven for 30 minutes. Remove and cool for 1 hour. Remove the string and allow the roast to cool to room temperature.

Using a very sharp knife, carefully cut into ½-inch slices and place on a bed of lettuce decorated with stuffed or whole green olives, ripe avocado slices, and radish rosettes.

SERVES 5 TO 6

THE WEDDING PARTY

Posole

Hominy and Pork Stew

Jalisco's traditional meal-in-a-bowl is named after the hominy added to this hearty soup. Whole chickens and hefty joints of pork were simmered in a stock turned a rich orange-red by *chile chilacate*, a pepper that resembles a dried Anaheim pepper, except it's hotter. A steaming bowl of *posole* is garnished with sliced radishes, diced onions, sliced cabbage, and a few squirts of lemon. This combination soup-salad-stew, which reminds me of Vietnamese Pho, was then heaped on crackly sun-dried tostadas painted with an incredibly hot, curry-like serrano chile paste. It's the perfect party feast. It can be served either sit-down or buffet-style. But like any good party, preparations can begin a day ahead by giving your tortillas a day in the sun. Trust us. Sun-dried tortillas fry into tostadas strong enough to hold juicy hunks of pork that won't crumble on your lap.

TOSTADAS
5 dozen corn tortillas
1 cup peanut oil
CONTINUED ON NEXT PAGE↝

SOUP

3 pounds pork ribs, cut into groups
  of 2 or 3 ribs
4 pounds pork shoulder, deboned and cut
  into 3-inch cubes
3 pounds turkey drumettes
2 tablespoons minced garlic
4 bay leaves
5 teaspoons salt
1 teaspoon cumin seeds
7 quarts water

HOMINY

7-½ quarts water
5 pounds uncooked *nixtamal*, rinsed twice
  (or 5 pounds canned white hominy if
  nixtamal is not available)
5 garlic cloves

CHILE PASTE

6 *guajillo* chiles, washed, seeded, and deveined
1 dozen dried *chilacate*, or dried California
  chiles, washed, seeded, and deveined
5 *puya* chiles if available, washed, seeded,
  and deveined
10 cups hot water
1 teaspoon white wine vinegar
5 tablespoons peanut oil

GARNISHES

1 head romaine lettuce, shredded
½ head white cabbage, shredded
3 cucumbers, peeled and sliced
2 medium yellow onions, chopped fine
6 lemons, cut into wedges
4 bunches radishes, sliced thin

To Make Tostadas:
We recommend that you sun-dry the tortillas
a day ahead of time. The temperature should
be above 80 degrees with low humidity.
Remove the tortillas from their plastic package, and deal them out side by side like playing
cards on a cloth-covered table. Make sure the
drying area receives full sun throughout the
day. Cover the tortillas with some cheesecloth.
This will protect the tortillas from unwanted
visitors and prevent them from warping.
Begin drying the tortillas as early as 9 A.M.,
since they will need to dry a good 6 to 7 hours.

Attractively arrange the garnishings on a large
platter. Place the platter where your guests
can help themselves to their favorite vegetable
toppings.

Bring the tortillas indoors. Heat 1 cup peanut oil in a medium skillet over a medium flame for about 5 minutes. Sauté one tortilla at a time until they turn a rich cinnamon brown. Firmly press the tortillas into the oil with a metal spatula to ensure that each stays flat. Drain on paper towels. You may choose to lightly salt each tortilla as they are stacked on a paper towel. Don't be alarmed if the tostadas have shrunken a bit—the sun-drying and frying have removed their moisture. Set aside in a dry place.

To Prepare the Posole:
You'll need two large kettles with tight-fitting lids. The *posole* meat and stock will cook in one kettle; the *nixtamal*, or limed-cooked corn, will cook in the other.

In kettle #1, place the meat, garlic, bay leaves, 3 teaspoons salt, cumin seed, and 7 quarts water. Bring to a boil, cover, reduce heat to low, and simmer for 2 hours.

In kettle #2, cook the whole *nixtamal* (hominy kernels) and garlic in 7-½ quarts water and simmer over a low flame for 2 hours. (Omit this step if using precooked canned hominy.)

To Prepare Chile Paste:
As the two kettles simmer, prepare the chile paste by rinsing, seeding, deveining, and sautéeing the chile skins in 5 tablespoons peanut oil. Place the chile skins in a large mixing bowl and soak them with 1 teaspoon vinegar and enough warm water to submerge them for 2 hours. Grind the soaked chile skins and about ¾ cup soaking solution in a blender, and set aside. (Consider grinding the chile skins in smaller amounts if blender is not large enough to hold all of them.)

To Assemble Posole:
After the 2 hours of cooking time are up, drain the cooked *nixtamal* and add it to the kettle containing the meat and stock. (If you are using canned white hominy, you may add it at this point. Rinse the hominy a few times before adding to the broth.) Pour in half of the chile paste, the remaining 2 teaspoons salt, and stir gently. Bring the broth to a boil and reduce heat to low. Taste the broth. You may choose to add more chile paste at this point, if you prefer a spicier broth. Cover the kettle and simmer for 25 minutes.
SERVES 12

Chile Serrano para Tostadas

Green Serrano Chile

This chile's so hot, you'll cry with pain, then joy, wondering how you'd lived without it. Make it a day ahead, as this allows time for the flavors to blend. You can store it in a glass jar with a tight-fitting lid in your refrigerator for up to 3 months.

1 pound fire-roasted serrano chiles
6 garlic cloves, roasted and peeled
3 teaspoons marjoram, fresh or dry
15 whole black peppercorns
12 whole allspice
17 whole cloves
½ cup plain white vinegar
2 teaspoons salt
1 cup water

PREPARATION
Preheat broiler. Rinse the chiles and dry with a paper towel. Place the chiles on a large cookie sheet. Roast 5 inches from the broiler, turning the chiles by shaking the cookie sheet every few minutes. Remove after 5 to 10 minutes or when the skins are slightly blistered and charred. Do not peel as their blackened skin adds to this chile's flavor. Cut stems off with a knife.

Place chiles in a blender with garlic, marjoram, peppercorns, allspice, cloves, and blend for 3 minutes at a slow speed. Add vinegar, salt, and water and blend at high speed 30 seconds longer. Pour the chile in a large glass or stainless-steel bowl and let it set a few hours before serving to allow the flavors to blend.

To Serve with the Posole:
Ladle the hot broth, *posole*, and meat into a bowl, garnish with ¼ cup lettuce or cabbage, ½ teaspoon onion, 3 slices cucumber, radish slices, and a few squeezes of a lemon wedge. Spread a spoonful of chile on a tostada. Spoon a few chunks of meat onto the tostada. Intersperse bites from the tostada with mouthfuls of soup and vegetables.

Mole Verde

Green Pork Mole

MEAT

3 pounds pork sirloin, trim excess fat
1 quart water
½ small white onion
1 garlic clove
2 bay leaves
2 teaspoons salt

TOMATILLOS

2 quarts water
2 pounds raw unhusked *tomatillos*
    (reserve 1 cup cooking liquid)
1 garlic clove, halved
½ teaspoon salt

MOLE SAUCE

Cooked, husked *tomatillos*
½ cup toasted pumpkin seeds for mole
½ cup toasted pumpkin seeds for garnish
4 large raw serrano chiles, roasted,
    sweated, peeled, seeded, and deveined
2 garlic cloves, roasted and peeled
10 *cilantro* sprigs for mole
10 *cilantro* sprigs for garnish
10 cumin seeds
1 leafy sprig *epazote*, or mint
10 coriander seeds
1 tortilla sautéed till golden in 1 teaspoon
    olive oil
2 tablespoons olive oil
1-½ cups fresh peas or frozen baby peas
Cooked pork
1 cup pork broth

PREPARATION

Place the pork sirloin in a large kettle, add
1 quart cold water, onion, garlic, bay leaves,
and salt. Bring to a boil, cover, and simmer
over a low flame for 40 minutes. Remove the
meat, cool, and cut into 1" x 1" stewing cubes.
Strain the broth through a sieve, and set aside.

Bring 2 quarts water to boil in a 3-quart
pot, add the unhusked *tomatillos*, garlic, and
salt and blanch for 3 minutes. Reserve 1 cup
 of the *tomatillo* broth before quickly pouring
the *tomatillos* into a colander to drain and cool.
Remove the *tomatillos*' outer husks by gently

CONTINUED ON NEXT PAGE⤸

pulling them back from the fruit and twisting them off from the stem. The *tomatillos* should not become mushy from overcooking.

Blend *tomatillos*, pumpkin seeds, serrano chiles, garlic, *cilantro*, cumin, *epazote* or mint sprigs, to a chunky consistency for 1 minute. Add the toasted tortilla to the green *tomatillo* sauce inside the blender, and quickly blend until smooth. You may need to add 1 or 2 tablespoons of the *tomatillo* broth to make sure the sauce does not gum up the blender's blades.

In a large skillet, heat 2 tablespoons of olive oil over a medium flame. Vigorously sauté the green mole sauce for 1 minute. Add the peas and pork to the mole and cook for 10 minutes, or until peas are tender and the sauce has thickened to a nice consistency. Add pork broth if the mole has become too thick. Add salt as needed. Garnish each serving with 1 teaspoon toasted pumpkin seeds and 2 or 3 *cilantro* sprigs. Serve with hot corn tortillas.

SERVES 6

OTHER HACIENDA RECIPES

Conejo en Huerto
Rabbit in the Garden

With recipes like "Rabbit in the Garden," Trinidad transformed whatever rabbit came her way into a poem of unusual sweet-and-sour flavors by stewing young rabbits in a tomato sauce flavored with tropical fruits and pickled vegetables.

BROTH
1 medium rabbit, cut into chunks
½ medium white onion, quartered
2 garlic cloves
1 bay leaf
½ teaspoon salt
6 cups water

STEW

4 tablespoons flour

3 tablespoons olive oil

1 garlic clove, minced

1 medium white onion, cut into
¼-inch-thick rings

2 medium tomatoes, chopped

2 teaspoons salt

4 cups strained rabbit or chicken broth,
plus ¼ cup

2 tablespoons blanched, peeled, and
halved almonds

3–4 pickled yellow chiles

¼ cup raisins

¾ cup green pitted olives

1 large quince, cut into wedges

1 large green apple (Gravenstein or
Granny Smith), cut into wedges

1 large ripe plantain (8 to 9 inches long),
cut diagonally into ¼-inch slices

¼ cup pickled cauliflower

¼ cup pickled carrots

PREPARATION

Heat a small saucepan over a medium flame. Pour 4 tablespoons flour into the pan, stirring steadily with a wooden spoon to prevent burning, until the flour takes on a golden color. Set aside.

Place the rabbit, onion, garlic, bay leaf, and salt in a large kettle with 6 cups cold water and bring to a boil, cover, and simmer for 40 to 45 minutes. Remove the rabbit, and set aside. Strain 4-¼ cups of broth, and set aside.

Heat the olive oil in a large skillet over a medium flame. Sauté the garlic for 30 seconds before adding the onion and tomato. Sauté for 3 minutes. Add salt, 4 cups broth (reserve ¼ cup), almonds, chiles, raisins, olives, quince, and the cooked rabbit. Cover and simmer for 20 minutes.

Add apple, plantain, pickled cauliflower, and carrots. In a small mixing bowl combine the browned flour and ¼ cup reserved broth and stir until the flour is completely dissolved, then pour into the stew and stir. Cover and simmer another 5 minutes. Be careful not to overcook the plantain and apples. Serve with rice. SERVES 6

Tamales de Telitas de Sayula

Sayula-Style Rolled Bean Tamales
Wrapped in Avocado Leaves

This recipe, practically a museum piece, was given to us by Ana Ugarte. Her tamale recipe of clearly pre-Hispanic origins, probably Tarascan, has a secret ingredient: the avocado leaf in which the tamale is rolled. You'll need the leaves from a Mexican seedling avocado; they have a subtle, smoky flavor that tastes of anise and green tea. They aren't rare in Southern California. You can find them growing in thousands of Latino backyards. Check if you've got a seedling variety by crushing a leaf in your hands. The fragrance is unmistakable. If the leaves from a Mexican seedling avocado tree are not available, you'll have to settle for corn husks.

STEP-BY-STEP PEN AND INK DRAWINGS OF HOW TO ASSEMBLE *Tamales de telitas de Sayula*, OR ROLLED TAMALES, BY LUCENA VALLE

½ cup olive oil
½ cup chopped yellow onions
7 whole *chile japonés* peppers
3 garlic cloves, crushed
½ cup diced ripe tomatoes
4 cups freshly cooked pinto beans
    (reserve ¼ cup bean broth)
1 teaspoon salt
5 pounds prepared *masa* (see Index)
24 seedling avocado leaves, rinsed
1 pound package corn husks, soaked in
    hot water for 3 hours; remove silk,
    rinse in cold water, and drain
1 16" x 26" cotton dish towel

PREPARATION

In a large skillet, heat the olive oil over a medium flame. Add the onions, peppers, garlic, and tomatoes. Sauté for 3 minutes, then thoroughly mash them with the back of a wooden spoon or bean masher. Add drained beans and salt. Heat for about 10 minutes, then puree the beans with a bean masher. Add ¼ cup bean broth and heat for another 15 minutes; cool and set aside.

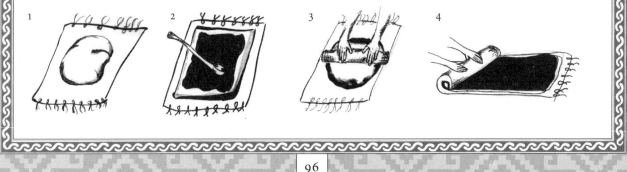

Prepare to roll up the tamales by spreading a 16"x 26" cotton damp dish towel on a large cookie sheet. Cover the cloth with 2-½ cups *masa*. Spread the *masa* with a pastry roller over the cloth to a thickness of ½ inch, stopping ½ inch short of the cloth's edges. Take 2 cups of pureed beans and spread over the *masa* in a ¼-inch-thick layer.

Carefully roll the dish towel from the widest side as if making a jelly roll. (Keep the tamale snug as you roll while pulling back the cloth from the *masa*. You don't want to roll the towel into the roll of *masa* and beans.) Repeat the procedure to make another rolled tamale.

Chill the rolled tamale in the freezer for 10 minutes to make slicing it easier. With twine or a very sharp knife, slice the tamale at 2-inch intervals, which should produce about a dozen individual rolls. Place each sliced roll in the center of a large corn husk. *Note*: Not all the corn husks will be wide enough to wrap each tamale completely, so you may have to spread 2 or 3 husks side by side. Wrap 1 avocado leaf around the circumference of each roll, then finish wrapping the roll in the corn husks, snugly tying off each end with thin strips of corn husk. Make the tamale ties by shredding the longest corn husks into thin strips. Hand-tied tamales will give you the prettiest bundles. Kitchen string cut in 6-inch lengths makes an adequate substitute. Steam the tamales for about 60 minutes in a large steamer.

Note: The tamales are *not* to be placed in the water itself, but in the steaming rack above the pot, which should be filled with about 4 inches of water. (Mexican grocery stores sell specially designed pots for steaming tamales. Chinese dim sum steamers also do well.) Bring the steamer to a boil and carefully arrange the tamales side by side. The tamales are ready when the *masa* slides off the corn husk. This recipes makes about 20 to 24 tamales.

The tamales can be stored in the freezer for up to 3 months. These tamales may be reheated in a 350-degree oven for 25 to 30 minutes.

SERVES 10 TO 12

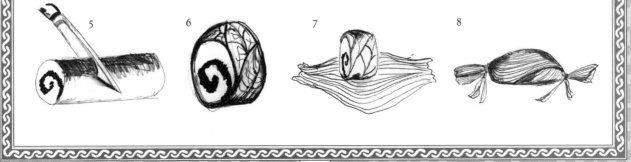

5   6   7   8

Sopa de Huescalapa

Huescalapa Soup

This isn't one of Trinidad's recipes, but it's such an extraordinary example of Jalisco's hacienda cookery I couldn't bear to leave it out. María Verea de Laird, a descendant of one of Jalisco's old landowning families, dictated it to me in her daughter's living room. The soup takes its name from her family's hacienda deep in southern Jalisco. María remembered it as a kind of coming home soup, one that told her the season as well as who she was. She tasted all of this in one spoonful: the pungent, slightly bitter fire of charred poblano chiles contrasted with the sweetness of early corn, the smooth richness of fresh cream, ripe avocados, and squash blossoms so tender they melt in the mouth.

BROTH
1 gallon water
1 whole chicken, discard innards
1 clove garlic
1 teaspoon salt

SOUP
⅓ cup, plus 3 tablespoons olive oil
4 corn tortillas, cut into ⅛-inch strips
4 squash flowers, stem and pistils removed, sliced lengthwise thinly for soup
2 cups fresh corn kernels, sliced off the cob
1 large green poblano or New Mexico chile, roasted, sweated, peeled, seeded, and deveined, cut into thin strips
½ cup finely minced red onion
½ teaspoon salt
10 cups strained chicken broth
2 cups zucchini, julienned and blanched for 2 minutes
2 cups cooked and cubed chicken breast
⅓ cup *asadero* or *oaxaca* cheese, sliced into thin strips
⅓ cup *jocoque*, or crème fraîche
2 medium-size, ripe Haas avocados, peeled and cut into 1-inch cubes
2 squash flowers, stems and pistils removed, sliced lengthwise

PREPARATION

Rinse the chicken with cold water. In an 8-quart kettle, add 1 gallon of water, the chicken, garlic, and salt. Bring to a boil over a medium flame, reduce heat to low, cover with a tight-fitting lid, and simmer for 25 minutes. Remove kettle from stove, skim away any scum that rises to the surface, strain 10 cups of broth through a fine sieve, and set aside. Remove chicken, drain, and cool before deboning. Chop the breast meat into 2 cups bite-size cubes.

Heat ⅓ cup of olive oil in an 8-inch skillet over a medium flame. Fry tortilla strips until golden brown. Drain on a paper towel, and set aside.

Heat 3 tablespoons olive oil in a 14-inch skillet over a medium flame. Sauté the squash blossoms, corn kernels, chile strips, and onion for 4 minutes. Season the sautéed vegetables with ½ teaspoon salt, and set aside. Assemble the soup by pouring in the 10 cups of broth into a 2-quart soup pot with a tight-fitting lid. Add the sautéed vegetable mixture, julienned zucchini, and cubed chicken meat. Cover and simmer over a low flame for 15 minutes. Remove the soup from the stove, and pour in the cheese. Slowly stir in the cream, followed by the cubed avocado. Return the pot to the stove and simmer over a very low flame for 5 minutes. Do not let the soup boil. Pour into a tureen and carry it to the table. Garnish each bowl with a few fried tortilla strips and a few shredded squash blossoms. SERVES 6

Helado de Zapote

Zapote Ice Cream

The pleasure of sliding her tongue over the creamy sweetness of exotic fruit ice creams was María's other reward for the long train and carriage ride to Huescalapa. It didn't matter that this was a yearly ritual. To María, the miracle of ice brought all the way down from the summit of a snow-capped volcano never lost its magic. She knew this was her father's gift to her, as extravagant as it may seem, and that made it special. He would hire men and mules days ahead to go up the icy shoulders of the 12,500-foot-high Colima Volcano rising from the surrounding jungles to haul down big blocks of ice.

"They'd bring down ice from the volcano, and they'd dig a deep pit, which they lined with tule mats" to keep it as cool as possible. "And then they'd bring the ice cream man all the way from Guadalajara so he could make ice cream right there. Just for our family. It was another world." The *zapote blanco*, or white *zapote*, is the only variety presently available in the United States. The fruit, which grows the size and shape of a large plum, is a light lime color and ripens like an avocado. Its cream-colored flesh blends a pleasant bitterness with sweet nut, vanilla, and pineapple flavors. CONTINUED ON NEXT PAGE⮑

Although grown in Southern California backyard gardens for years, it's now being harvested commercially there and in Hawaii, and is distributed to a select number of supermarkets. Your best option for obtaining fresh *zapotes* is from a mail order fruit distributor. (See Appendix B.)

5 pounds ripe *zapotes*, peeled, seeded, and pureed in a blender or food processor (makes 4 cups)
3 cups sugar
¾ cup water
2-inch vanilla stick
½ quart half-and-half

PREPARATION
In a 2-quart kettle, mix sugar and water and boil for 5 minutes. Add 4 cups pureed *zapote* and a vanilla stick, and simmer for an additional 10 minutes. Remove the kettle from the stove and allow its contents to cool. Add the half-and-half and blend thoroughly. Pour into the ice cream maker and follow the manufacturer's instructions.
SERVES 6

Nieve de Mango, Naranja, y Plátano

Mango-Orange-Banana Ice Cream

4 large mangoes, seeded and pureed (makes 4 cups)
3 cups freshly squeezed orange juice with pulp, seeds removed
1 ripe banana, pureed
1 cup sugar
1 cup half-and-half

PREPARATION
Mix all the ingredients in a large bowl, pour into the ice cream maker, and follow the manufacturer's directions.
SERVES 5 TO 6

FROM THE LAKE

Pescado Blanco Relleno
Stuffed Whitefish

Trinidad's recipe for paper-wrapped fish out-shines all the others by introducing the briny ocean to a sweet water lake. The most practical substitute for a Chapala whitefish is a rainbow trout or pan-size salmon. But any mild-tasting, white-fleshed fish should prove just as satisfying. Save yourself time and fuss. Ask your fish seller to debone the fish.

BROTH
2 cups cold water
1-½ pounds jumbo, unshelled shrimp
1 garlic clove
¼ teaspoon salt

STUFFING
4 rainbow trout, 12 inches long
3 tablespoons olive oil
1 teaspoon chopped garlic
½ cup finely diced white onion
2-½ cups finely diced tomato
⅓ teaspoon cinnamon
¼ teaspoon ground clove
⅓ cup finely chopped green olives
3–4 small yellow pickled chiles, halved
5 tablespoons shrimp stock
⅓ cup dry white wine

¾ teaspoon salt
¼ cup soft butter
5 cups day-old sourdough bread crumbs
½ cup peanut or olive oil
3 lemons, cut into wedges
10 sprigs Italian parsley

EQUIPMENT
1 large upholstery needle
3 yards parchment paper
1 spool cooking string

Deboning: With a very sharp knife, cut the rib bones of the trout along a line closest to the right side of the spinal column all the way down to the tail fins. Repeat the procedure for the left side. Carefully clip the spinal vertebrae free of the tail fins and the head. The trout should splay open. Now gently run the knife blade behind the spinal column and separate the flesh from the dorsal spines. Be careful not to cut through the skin as this will slice the fish in two. Slowly pull the spinal column away with a pair of pliers or fish tweezers. Gently scrape the rib bones at the point where they were clipped from the spinal column with the blade-edge of a knife until they protrude a bit. Pull the rib bones out one by one with tweezers. Return the fish to the refrigerator. CONTINUED ON NEXT PAGE ↪

BROTH:

Pour 2 cups water into a 5-quart soup pot, bring it to a boil, add the unshelled shrimp, garlic, and salt. Reduce the heat to medium and simmer for 3 to 4 minutes. Remove the shrimp, cool, peel, and chop into chunks. Save the broth.

STUFFING:

Heat 3 tablespoons olive oil in a 14-inch skillet over a medium flame. Quickly sauté the minced garlic and onions. Add the tomato and sauté for 5 minutes, or until the tomatoes soften. Add cinnamon, clove, shrimp, olives, chiles, stock, wine, and salt, then simmer until the liquid in the stuffing is cooked off.

Spoon in about 4 or more tablespoons of stuffing inside the cavity of each deboned fish. Thread the needle with a 15-inch length of cooking string, knot the string, and carefully sew the fish closed. Rub the fish with generous amounts of butter, then roll it in bread crumbs. Cut enough parchment paper to wrap one fish twice over. Butter the side of the paper that will touch the fish. Wrap the fish up in the paper firmly tying off each end with a bit of string. Repeat the procedure for each fish. Preheat oven to 150 degrees. Pour ½ cup peanut oil into a 14-inch skillet and heat over a medium flame until very hot. Fry the fish for 10 minutes on each side. Add peanut oil as required. A rich aroma of shrimp and toasted bread will indicate when the fish is cooked.

Lift each fish with metal tongs and drain on paper towel. Put the wrapped fish on a large cookie sheet. Keep warm in oven until serving time. Remove the parchment paper, snip away string, and promptly serve the fish on a platter with parsley sprigs and lemon wedges.

SERVES 6

Bagre Relleno
Stuffed Catfish

2 tablespoons olive oil
2 poblano chiles, roasted, sweated, peeled, seeded, deveined, chopped
4 Anaheim chiles roasted, sweated, peeled, seeded, deveined and chopped
7 cloves, ground fine
3 garlic cloves, minced
1 cup chopped tomato
½ cup chopped Italian parsley
3 large hard-cooked egg yolks, chopped
½ teaspoon salt
¼ teaspoon black pepper
2 tablespoons extra virgin olive oil for stuffing
3 medium channel catfish, deboned
1 tablespoon soft butter
½ teaspoon salt
2 cups sourdough bread crumbs
1-½ cups peanut oil

EQUIPMENT
1 large upholstery needle
1 yard parchment paper
1 spool cooking string

Heat 2 tablespoons olive oil in a large skillet over a medium flame. Sauté the chopped chiles, cloves, garlic, tomatoes, and parsley. Stir in the chopped eggs, salt, pepper, a bit more olive oil as needed. Cook the stuffing down to a pasty consistency, remove the skillet from the stove, and set aside.

Preheat oven to 150 degrees. Rub the cavity of each fish with butter, then fill with the stuffing and sew up each fish. Rub the outside of each fish with the remaining butter and ½ teaspoon salt, then dredge each fish in bread crumbs. Cut a sheet of parchment paper large enough to wrap each fish twice over. Wrap the fish and tie off each end of the parchment paper with string. Trim away the excess paper so that each fish fits in the skillet. Heat 1-½ cups peanut oil in a 14-inch skillet over a medium flame until very hot. Fry each fish for 3 minutes on each side. Lift the wrapped fish with metal tongs, allowing the excess oil to drain back into the skillet. Place the fish on a large cookie sheet, then keep warm in oven until serving time. Right before serving remove the parchment paper, snip away the cooking string, and serve immediately with the following salsa.

SERVES 6

Salsa para Pescado

Chapala-Style Salsa

5 *cascabel* chiles, washed, seeded, and deveined
2 *chiles arboles*, whole
1 large garlic clove, roasted and peeled
1 tablespoon white onion, roasted and diced
1-½ teaspoons salt
½ teaspoon allspice
2 large tomatoes, roasted and quartered
1 tablespoon warm water
1 teaspoon rice wine vinegar
1 tablespoon olive oil
1 dozen *cilantro* sprigs, minced

Heat a heavy skillet over a medium flame and toast the chiles for 30 seconds until the skins turn a dark red. Set aside. Place the garlic, onion, and salt in a food processor or blender and grind to a coarse consistency (see Appendix). Add the allspice and chiles and continue grinding until well blended. Add the tomatoes and grind them to a pulpy consistency. Pour the sauce into a serving bowl. Rinse the container with 1 tablespoon of warm water, making sure to pour any left-over salsa into the sauce bowl. Stir in the vinegar, olive oil, and *cilantro*.

Pescado Robalo

Bass in a Clemole Sauce

Trinidad's recipe works well with both salt and freshwater species. She recommended cod if bass was not available. She dresses up the fish with a *clemole*, a simple roast tomato-chile *ancho* sauce.

1 ½ cups tomato, roasted, peeled, and ground
1 *chile ancho*, washed, seeded, and deveined, soaked for 30 minutes in 1 cup hot water and 1 teaspoon of vinegar (reserve ½ cup soaking solution)
2 large garlic cloves, roasted and peeled
½ teaspoon white pepper
4 whole allspice
1 teaspoon salt
1 whole 2- to 2-½-pound bass or rock cod, cleaned, scaled, and dried
2 tablespoons flour
⅓ cup olive oil, plus 3 tablespoons
⅓ cup lard

Place the roasted tomato, soaked *chile ancho* skins, garlic, white pepper, ½ cup soaking solution, allspice, and salt in a blender or food processor, and grind to a smooth paste. Rinse out the remaining chile paste with a few tablespoons of soaking solution. Set aside.

Preheat oven to 150 degrees. Dry fish thoroughly with paper towels. Score the bass with three shallow diagonal cuts on each side and lightly dredge in flour. Heat ⅓ cup olive oil and ⅓ cup lard in a 14-inch skillet over a high flame. Fry fish on both sides for 5 minutes each, or until the fins are crispy. Drain fish on paper towel and place on an attractive heat-resistant platter. Keep fish in oven while preparing the sauce.

Heat 3 tablespoons olive oil in a 12-inch saucepan over a hot flame, reduce heat to medium, pour in the *clemole* and sizzle it 4 minutes. Remove the fish from the oven, cover it with the sauce, and serve.
SERVES 4 TO 5

hard times befall the san felipe inn

Inns similar to the San Felipe began their decline the day the steam engines rolled into Guadalajara. The automobile finished the job more than four decades later. Today, the only vestiges of these establishments are their massive adobe walls and high arched gateways. But instead of being crowded with carriages and wagons, the old inn courtyards have become parking lots for automobiles.

Back in May 1888, however, when the first box cars rolled into Guadalajara, most people, including Catalina, saw the railroad as a symbol of progress. The local papers promised that the dangers and vagaries of shipping people and goods over poorly maintained, bandit-infested highways would fade into the past. Now their city was efficiently connected to the nation's capital, and someday, the northern border states. New Orleans oysters, Norwegian cod, fresh red snappers shipped in ice from the Gulf of Mexico, apples and butter from California, potatoes from Colorado, even barrels of Milwaukee beer would arrive by train. No one seemed to care that the *norteamericanos* who owned the rails, and the English textile barons who used them, could now make new demands, culinary and otherwise, upon Guadalajara and its residents. Although English and Anglo-American cooking was at least two centuries old in Mexico, the city's growing English-speaking business community won new admirers for pink roast beef, boiled potatoes, apple pie, or club sandwiches. Although not entirely reputable, private clubs such as the German Casino, the English Casino, and the American Casino became the point of entry for new food fashions started by Guadalajara's growing foreign business community. For example, at El Casino Español, where my grandfather later worked as its accountant, my father got his first taste of a club sandwich, which, with its bland white bread and American cheese, seemed to him an exotic delicacy.

The new merchants and the businesses they managed also increased the number and variety of Guadalajara's hotels and restaurants. Downtown, Remigio Lions, the proprietor of The French Candy and Pastry Shop, advertised French wines, liquor, fruit preserves, French-style tortes, and vol-au-vent, the light, steamy pastry shells filled with chicken, which the fork startles into flight when it pierces its delicate crust. Another establishment, The Italian Fame, advertised Italian wines, olive oil, pastas, Italian cheeses, sausages, canned goods, and glassware. From Wednesday to Sunday, an eatery called The Central Street Restaurant and Saloon served up such Spanish standards as *Olla Podrida*, literally Rotten Pot, a bountiful stew of various stewed meats and vegetables from which Cassoulet was derived, and *Bacalao a la Vizcaina*, or Basque-style Salt Cod. Pastries and ice cream were the restaurant's featured desserts. Spanish-style pork sausages such as *salchichón* sold for thirty-seven cents a pound. And, in a bid for the respectability the inns could not guarantee, the restaurant assured its guests that "persons who find themselves in a state of inebriation will be barred from entering the dining room."

Inevitably, the inns became irrelevant. Businessmen and tourists now patronized the restaurants and hotels, and more and more goods came into Guadalajara by train. That meant that the muleteers who once made the nation's economy

PRODUCT ADVERTISEMENTS PUBLISHED IN THE 1888 EDITIONS OF *JUAN PANADERO*, A GUADALAJARA NEWSPAPER.

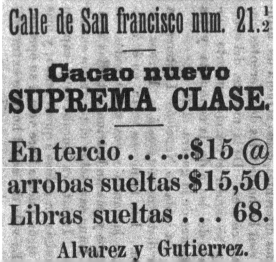

move had fewer goods to haul. Meanwhile, a more sophisticated tourist began to prefer the meals and comforts offered by the new hotels. Even the godfathers to Gregorio's children, the hat maker and the tailor who regularly dropped in for a drink or meal, suddenly found themselves competing with merchandise shipped in from the factories and textile mills of El Salto, Tepíc, or Sayula.

The San Felipe Inn held out longer than most. Mention of the San Felipe appears as late as 1945. Trinidad's ties to the inn, however were cut prematurely when her husband died in 1898. She could no longer afford the comfortable, though modest life her husband had provided.

To make matters worse, her daughter, María, had lost her husband a few years earlier in 1896. Trinidad, María, and her daughter, Delfina, thus had little choice but to prevail upon Catalina's generosity to share her living quarters at 496 Calle Liceo. Needless to say, the houseful of women lived a spartan existence on Catalina's headmistress salary. Delfina, for her part, felt herself orphaned inside the spacious two-story school ruled by Catalina. Delfina suspected that Catalina had instructed her teachers to be especially stern with her, believing her aunt did not want the other students. Afterward, Delfina came to appreciate the way her aunt instilled in her the confidence and independence to act alone.

Trinidad, however, lacked the resiliency of Delfina's youth. She died in 1918, never quite having accepted her widowhood. One family story has it that she would cover her shopping basket with her *chal* when she made her early morning visit to the marketplace. You see, she did not want her neighbors to know that she no longer had servants to do her shopping.

As it turned out, her husband's death foreshadowed the decline of Guadalajara's inns, Trinidad's loss of status, and decades of exile for her descendants, including Delfina, who would later orchestrate the feast of squab on saffron rice.

With her recipes in tow, Delfina would, in 1926, board a train headed north, where she joined Catalina's younger sister, Juanita, who, after fleeing *La Sauceda*, was waiting for her in Los Angeles.

Delfina's recipes arrived in Los Angeles in less than favorable circumstances. Low wages, long hours, and a scarcity of ingredients made it almost impossible for her to prepare the elaborate city-bred recipes she'd learned in Guadalajara. She also came to conquered territory, land that once belonged to her ancestors, a fact that had already altered the meaning and making of her cuisine. Still, Delfina came with certain advantages. In addition to Juanita's family, and her recipes, she had faith in the written word with which to summon her memories across the border. More than once, Catalina and Trinidad would appear like ghosts to help Delfina and her descendants survive in their new home—California.

PART TWO

California

and Its New Mestizo Culture

reinventing home

THE LETTERS HER AUNT MAILED FROM LOS Angeles lured Delfina across the border. Juanita, Catalina's younger sister, wrote to Delfina of jobs that paid more than a dollar a day milking cows, picking oranges, laying track, digging ditches, sewing shirt collars . . . jobs that paid only pennies a day in Mexico.

The real experiences of Delfina's husband, Pablo, confirmed the stories the letters told. Several years earlier, while working as a federal postal clerk, he would sort letters in mailbags he dropped off along his route, from Guadalajara to Mexicali. He must have felt like a dealer giving away the best cards, since he could detect from an envelope's thickness that dollars were enclosed. The addresses named the families in Guadalajara who bought sewing machines and radios, the factory-made goods Pablo could barely afford on his fixed salary; a salary diminished by debts that mounted with each of his failed business ventures—first a soap factory, then a shoemaking

operation. Their financial difficulties worsened until they were forced to mortgage their home to pay off debts. They didn't know it then, but private and economic chaos combined to loosen their attachments to Guadalajara, and to each other.

Delfina had her own reasons for going. In 1909, at the age of seventeen, she married a man almost twice her age expecting the modest comforts of middle-class life. She lived the dream for a time. Pablo's salary as a postal clerk meant Delfina could afford to cook Trinidad's recipes and hire a servant. But then, in 1920, Pablo lost his government job. His surviving children say Pablo was dimissed because he refused to renounce his loyalty to the church, which a paranoid federal government suspected of fomenting counterrevolution in the state of Jalisco. Whatever the reason, Pablo's dismissal triggered a rapid decline. Delfina now struggled to maintain a middle-class household on her husband's sporadic wages. Motherhood proved to be its own ordeal. The first five children Delfina bore all died. High child mortality rates were the norm then, even in cities, where newborns were threatened by persistent hunger, unsanitary water supplies, and infectious diseases. Although Delfina never expressed her despair to her four surviving children, her daughter Estela said she's certain her mother suffered these losses just as she'd suffered her own son's death many years later.

Not surprisingly, the urge to leave momentarily overcame Delfina and Pablo. Staying meant being reduced to déclassé oblivion. If they had to sell their home and take up menial wage labor, better to submit far from home where no one could see them.

"'Fine,'" Estela remembers overhearing her father say. "'Delfina, you take the children. I'll catch up with you as soon as I sell the house.'"

Pablo paid for the train tickets, including one for a male cousin who escorted his wife and children, from what he earned bookkeeping for El Casino Español, a fancy gaming club for Spanish businessmen. In a previous century, Pablo would have considered himself lucky to have such a job, but not in the mid-1920s. Salaries had not changed since 1900, though the cost of living had increased as much as seventy-fold.

Between 1910 and 1929, fleeing war and poverty, more than a million Mexicans streamed north across the Rio Bravo into the southwestern United States. By 1920, as much as 20 percent of the population of Los Angeles County was Mexican. Most came from the western states, like Jalisco, fleeing overpopulated, unproductive haciendas, a war-ravaged economy, and the government's brutal suppression of the Cristero peasant revolt, instigated by fanatical country priests who hoped to reverse the revolution's anticlerical reforms. Droughts lasting until the 1930s finished the job, sending still more people north.

Despite the scale of the exodus, most didn't expect to stay long. They'd seek safety and money in California, then return. But once drawn into the vortex, these fragments of families discovered the other Mexicos they barely knew existed. And so a new community fabric was woven. Immigrants from Jalisco enmeshed with ranching families from Chihuahua or Sonora, commencing a new cycle of *mestizaje*. Exile became a rebirth, one that required forgetting enough of the past to improvise their new selves, piecing together something new from old, odd remnants. Delfina stitched herself to this new life.

At her first job in Los Angeles, sorting rags, Delfina found herself shoulder to shoulder with women she would have hired as maids in Guadalajara. And they knew it. They took pleasure in denying her the deference to which she was accustomed. She remembered them as hard, foulmouthed, ready to anger. After the first day, she returned to her aunt's house in tears. Sorting rags was nothing like switching telephone calls, which she enjoyed as a young unmarried girl in Guadalajara, listening in on Jalisco's wealthy Tequila barons and their spoiled children. She considered giving up, going back. Then a letter written by Catalina's younger sister, Trinidad, arrived.

It said that Pablo had fathered a son with a maid named Felipa, a teenaged neighborhood girl. Trinidad urged Delfina to return and fight for what was rightfully hers—a place at her husband's side and what belongings remained from her former household. "All of this came as a great shock to my mother," Estela said. Pablo had given Delfina reasons for anger before. "My father liked to pinch the maids," Estela said. "Clearly, he was no saint. And they certainly had had their differences. She was married to a Mexican man, after all." But news of the child's birth gave Delfina grounds to break her agreement with Pablo. "It was only one, but that was enough," Estela said. "He'd gone too far."

DELFINA AND PABLO, A WEDDING POSE, CIRCA 1909.

Estela described Felipa as a tart who'd seduced her way into her father's house, ruling out, at least in her mind, the possibility that Felipa may have been a victim of an older man's lust. Delfina, for her part, considered Felipa's motives irrelevant. It was her husband, after all, who sold the house and squandered the profit on a stranger. But Delfina had distance in her favor. She was free enough, and far enough away, not to forgive him.

"So she decided to stay," Estella said, rather than return and reclaim her place as wife, as Trinidad suggested. "'I don't think I'll go back,'" Estela said, assuming her mother's voice. "My mother was by no means an ordinary woman."

The revolution of 1910, its wrenching economic aftermath, and the resulting separations of husbands from wives, broke up thousands of marriages. Spanish-language papers in Los Angeles regularly ran ads of wives asking for the whereabouts of wayward husbands. Pablo was simply one of many who'd stumbled. Delfina, for her part, did not remind her children of their father's indiscretion. Despite Delfina's deep disappointment, she continued to respect her husband's memory before her children.

That's why his children remember their father tall, aloof, handsome, and shrouded in a hazy softness. They chose to remember his romantic impracticality, his violin playing in the patio, his imperturbable patience, and his reluctance to scold. Above all, they remember the postcards and poems he sent them: the acknowledgment they craved as children. One poem, written to Estela on a postcard with red velvet roses, compares her beauty to astral brilliance, but with a subtle turn toward darkness:

May an aureola of good fortune and
　　happiness
Ilumine your placid existence,
May it dissipate the shadows of bitterness
And shield your soul with innocence.

The poem is dated August 14, 1928, about a year after Delfina had learned of Pablo's affair. He wrote another, this one to Delfina. It speaks of "a soul . . . captivated by pain," and "of a happiness/that takes wing to pursue you." The poem's intention survives cliché. I believe Pablo wrote the poem hoping for a reconciliation. But it would take more than verses to change Delfina's mind, or erase the memory of a betrayal.

Delfina's decision to stay in Los Angeles proved humbling. She could not find steady work after walking away from her rag-sorting job, so she had no choice but to move in with her aunt, Juanita, and her husband, José. Delfina's waning independence added a sense of desperation to her heartache.

Now "she fretted about becoming a burden to their family," Estela recalls. "She didn't know where to turn, where to find work. She was a stranger here." But she was too proud to go back.

Juanita understood Delfina's predicament, so she asked her sons to see what they could do. They secured one of the two-bedroom woodframe shacks provided to dairy workers with families. Now Delfina and the kids could have a place of their own, even if it was drafty and built on a flea-infested riverbed. Since the dairy gave Juanita's sons free room and board, they could afford to pay Delfina to cook their meals on a stove that flavored everything with a hint of kerosene. So the shack became a dining hall for Juanita's sons, who'd by now grown tired of fried chicken with mashed potatoes and gravy, and the other Americano foods the dairy cooked for its Mexican workers.

Other milkers quickly got wind of Delfina's cooking. During the work week, Delfina cooked for Juanita's sons and four other milkers. To meet the demands, Delfina kneaded and rolled out more than one hundred pounds of flour tortillas each week, and then found several more egg crates to seat her new guests. On these crates sat six men eager to pay a bit extra for thinly sliced steaks grilled with onions, refried beans spiked with chards of toasted *chilacate* chile and crumbled, homemade cheese; *sopa de fideos* in garlicky chicken broth, steaming columns of hand-rolled flour tortillas, and burnt-orange, pan-roasted *chile de árbol*. Not surprisingly, milk was plentiful, as was stringy beef from freshly slaughtered dairy cows.

On Sundays, friends and relatives came, bearing groceries so that they'd be sure to have a place at Delfina's table. Later, the *verdurero*, the produce peddler, might drive his truck to the ranch to bet on the rooster fights behind the corrals. Before betting, the vendor sold Delfina string beans, tomatoes, or serranos for that day's *guisado*—what we now call steak *picado*, a pan-fried and stewed combination of chopped steak, tomato, onion, garlic, and available vegetables. Fresh produce marked a special occasion. Big meaty Anaheims grown in San Fernando—roasted and stuffed with homemade cheese, coated and fried in beaten egg white—were served in a tomato sauce of sliced onions, dried oregano, and a few pickled chiles.

And if supplies ran low, there was always enough milk—at least ten gallons per family per week, more sometimes—for Delfina to run a small cheese-making operation. With the help of her children, she made *panela*, a simple hoop cheese best eaten fresh, *queso casero*, a salty cheese made for drying and aging and selling to other Mexican families, or the ultimate treat, *chongos en almibar*, fresh curd simmered in a cinammon- or citrus-flavored sugar syrup. From the whey left over from cheesemaking, they made *requesón*, a ricotta-like cheese.

In addition to feasting, Sundays were for attending mass and shopping. My father and Estela remember rattling into downtown Los Angeles in Rafael's hard-wheeled Model T. Their destination: Nuestra Señora de Los Angeles, the eighteenth-century Franciscan mission that presides over the plaza by the same name. After being closeted in flickering candles, florid perfumes, and perspired shirt collars, they stepped out across Main Street, once La Principal, to La Luz del Día, a dry goods store, and La Esperanza, a bakery catering to a growing Mexican population. In the plaza itself, local vendors sold fresh fruits and vegetables, hawked ears of roast corn, tacos, tamales, and barbecued beef heads from pushcarts, a reminder of their own village marketplaces. A few blocks away on Spring Street, La Nacional sold a variety of dried legumes, including black beans, lard in bulk, 100-pound sacks of whole white corn, several brands of wheat flour, and *ristras* of strung dried California chiles; everything, in other words, for those who made their tortillas and tamales at home.

The Grand Central Market on Broadway was the closest thing to a bustling communal marketplace. Besides its labyrinth of stalls piled high with fragrant fruits and vivid vegetables and aisles filled with haggling shoppers, the Grand Central was known for its fresh fish and so-called

variety cuts. Immigrant shoppers came for the thick cow's tongues, languid and speckled; glistening, convoluted cow's brains, marbled oxtails and pinkish pig's feet, white honeycombed tripe, jewel-like kidneys, stiff-clawed chicken feet, and other suspicious organ meats. Here immigrants could boast to each other of secret victories. Here *arrechera*, the belts of skirt steak girding a cow's voluminous intestines, was considered a cheap variety cut like kidneys or liver. (The early Californios prized the belts of fatty, tender muscle as the ideal range delicacy, since it was easy to

THE WATSON AVENUE MARKET IN LOS ANGELES OWNED BY JOSÉ RAMON MARES, CIRCA 1920S. LEFT TO RIGHT AT COUNTER, AURELIO GARIBAY, JOSEFINA MARES, NEXT FIGURE UNIDENTIFIED, JOSÉ MARES. TORTILLERÍA IN THE BACK. *Courtesy Security Pacific Collection/L.A. Public Library.*

remove after skinning, and easier to skewer over a fire.) Crates of dried *bacalao* (salt cod), popeyed cow cods, thick sea bass, halibut steaks ribboned in thick succulent skin, and inky tubs of squid, could always be had.

The goods came from Mexico, Latin America, and even Spain. On rail lines from Central Mexico boxcars hauled in *chile mulato, chile pasilla, chile ancho, chile guajillo*, mesquite-smoked *chile chipotle*, dried tamarind pods, *pinole* (ground and toasted corn to which milk can be added as a breakfast food), dried corn husks, and *piloncillo*, or cones of raw sugar. From the mountains of Sinaloa and Sonora came the incendiary round berrylike *chile piquín de bolita*, dried cooking and medicinal herbs, and whole unroasted coffee beans from southern Mexico. Baja supplied Los Angeles with various styles of dried beef, canned seafood, including pickled squid and eels, and Latin American trade goods unloaded on its docks at Ensenada; *chicharrones de vieja* (big, crunchy pork rinds), hand-churned butter wrapped in maize leaves, *panela, queso añejo* (a salty aged cheese), chile-spiced *queso enchilado* for enchiladas, and "Jijona" brand *turrón*, or Spanish-style nougat.

A handful of companies also packed Mexican foods locally. The Cotera Brothers ran a mail-order business out of El Paso that advertised Mexican chocolate, coffee, moles, and other dry foodstuffs in *La Opinión*, while La Victoria Packing Company advertised *Mole Poblano, Pipian Ranchero, Salsa del Diablo Rojo, Chilitos en Escabeche, Tomatillo* (presumably canned), *Salsa Serrana*, and *Cajeta de Membrillo* (candied quince). In 1906, Emilio C. Ortega moved his chile roasting operation from his father's home in Ventura to Los Angeles, where he founded the Ortega Chile Company, the first to develop a system for canning fire-roasted green chile. Del Monte, one of the first national canners, begins to advertise its Chile Verde Pelado, or canned and peeled green chile, by 1919 in *El Heraldo de México*. But Del Monte represented a rare exception of a national canning company producing a Mexican food product for a regional market. For the most part, the job of industrializing the production of Mexican foods and condiments was being carried out by a handful of pioneering Mexican business owners, like Rose Ramírez, who teamed up with Ernie Feraud in 1923 to establish the Ramírez & Feraud Chili Company, which specialized in red chile and enchilada sauces. But there was one essential part of her Central Mexican diet which Delfina could not buy while living at the dairy's labor camp—corn tortillas. For these she would have to wait until Sunday to go buy them in Los Angeles, where the demand was great enough to sustain a fledgling industry.

The Automated Tortilla: From Stone Age to Jet Age

The modern history of the tortilla began quite late. From about 1000 B.C. until about the 1930s, the technology of tortilla making had done quite well with simple Stone Age technology. Of course, iron griddles heated by gas and stone mills driven by gas-powered motors had made tortilla making a bit more convenient and efficient. But the process of turning maize into a pillar of civilization remained essentially unchanged.

Someone had to finish the time-consuming process of grinding the lime-cooked corn, or *nixtamal*, in a *metate* until smooth enough to pat into thin moist discs. They risked blistering fingertips when flipping the tortilla on the griddle, or when pressing the tortilla with a moist cloth to make sure the steam was trapped inside. The tortilla would puff up and the cooking process was completed. Tortilla making at this rate was a slow process.

Of course, there were inventors in Mexico who had, by the 1920s, succeeded in mechanizing the tortilla rolling, cutting, and baking process. But they hadn't figured out how to coordinate all three steps in a single operation. That crucial integrating moment occurred in Los Angeles in the early 1930s, says Mario Orozco, president of the Azteca Milling Company, and coordinator of the Golden Tortilla Award, a yearly event designed to recognize the Los Angeles-area's growing tortilla industry.

In 1933, according to Orozco, the Pérez family of Los Angeles patented an electrically powered device for rolling and cutting the tortillas, an innovation that standardized tortilla size and texture. A few years later, a Señor Bobadilla connected a rolling and cutting machine to a three-tiered conveyor belt consisting of heated metal plates. The device simultaneously baked and deposited the tortillas in a pile at the end of the conveyor belt.

But fully automatic machines based on Bobadilla's design did not go into commercial operation until 1942, when Rebecca and Mario Carranza opened the El Zarape Tortilla Factory at the corner of Jefferson and Arlington boulevards in southwest Los Angeles. The Carranzas bought five machines manufactured by a Señor Sáinz, who used the Bobadilla design, but with crucial improvements. Still, Sáinz had waited years to sell his machines, Orozco writes, because "no one wanted to eat tortillas made by a 'machine.'" The El Zarape Tortilla Factory put two of the Sáinz machines into production in 1942, but held one in reserve to avoid laying off *tortilleras*, Orozco said. Although temperamental, each machine produced quality tortillas at the phenomenal rate of 100 dozen an hour, which convinced the Carranzas to fire up their third machine.

MEXICAN WOMAN MAKING CORN TORTILLAS BY HAND AT THE EL SOL DE MAYO TORTILLA PLANT OWNED BY MARIA QUEVADO, 110 N. SPRING ST., CIRCA 1920S. *Courtesy Security Pacific Collection/L.A. Public Library.*

"The Electric Zarape Tortilla Factory, with its automatic machine, was so successful," writes Orozco, "that others quickly launched into the design and manufacture of improved tortilla machines." Since then, the increasing automation of tortilla making and the development of premixed cornmeal has created a more than $1 billion industry, which is now going global. Today, machine-made tortillas outsell bagels, and are stacked on supermarket shelves from Alaska to Maine, while Orozco jets overseas to set up mechanized tortilla making operations from Paris to Tokyo.

EVEN WITH THE ABUNDANCE AND VARIETY of imported dry goods, low milker's wages (about $45 a month in 1927) drastically limited Delfina's cooking options. She spent most of their money on such staples as flour, beans, rice, and so on. After all, her customers could only afford to pay her so much for meals. Beyond the staples, Delfina improvised. *Cilantro* was hard to get. Dried California (Anaheims) substituted for Jalisco's hotter *chilaca* pods; spinach replaced *romeritos*, a tiny wild herbal green. Fresh fruits such as plantain or mango were simply unobtainable.

Still, Delfina and her family could always count on a few seasonal delicacies. For a few weeks in late spring and early summer, tender, bright green *nopalitos*, or beavertail cactus leaves, burst forth from the arms of weathered opuntia, thorny markers planted decades earlier by preceding Mexicans. After removing their immature spines, diced and cooked *nopalitos* were traditionally simmered with *tortas de camarón*, small, pan-fried soufflés of dried pulverized shrimp held together by beaten egg whites. In late fall, after a season of good rains, the same beavertail cactus produced purple, crimson, and yellow-green *tunas* or prickly pears. Two persons holding a pair of dried mustard stalks partially disarmed the fruit of its fiberglass-like spines by rolling it on the grass. After rinsing and peeling, the *tunas* could be eaten whole, or seeded and blended into a refreshing drink, or cooked down into a candy.

Few Mexicans at that time owned land, which more or less precluded home gardening. Many lived in labor camps, often hidden from view by orange or lemon groves. The community's social invisibility allowed a lot of respectable folks to view Mexicans as foreigners. That they clung to this notion even as they dreamed of California as a "Spanish" Eden shouldn't seem odd. They had long swallowed the myth of "Spanish" romance, *sans* Mexicans.

Yet Delfina's son, Manuel, hardly recalls being shunned or deprived. Roger Jessup's dairy near Glandale gave him the supportive company of his uncles, and a chance to be a kid again. He loved squeezing warm milk from a cow he had tamed, then scrambling up a high mound of bakery surplus—broken cookies, almonds, dried figs, apples, apricots—piled high inside the dairy's feed barns. Reclining at the top of the mound, he would take his fill of milk and cookies and dried fruit destined for the feed troughs.

It was different for Delfina. "My mother suffered a lot," Estela recalls. "Can you imagine. From having known almost nothing about housework to washing men's work clothes by hand, to making them breakfast, lunch, and dinner. In Guadalajara she had maids to help her with everything." She staved off loneliness and despair by escaping into fiction. Each night, after having cleared the table, she waited for her audience to arrive—the milker's wives and her aunts and cousins—before she gave her dramatic readings of *Les Misérables* and other novels in installments.

Sopa de Fideos

Vermicelli Soup

Like those that follow it, this is a recipe remembered from Delfina's cooking, passed along and modified in our family from one generation to the next, what a mother taught a daughter or son. The cooking lesson usually came a few days before a mother began working nights. Delfina added sliced ripened plantain when she could get a hold of it.

3 tablespoons olive oil
3 garlic cloves, minced
4 ounces Mexican fideo, or fine vermicelli,
    broken up until pasta is unwound
1 ripe tomato, chopped
½ medium onion, chopped
3 cups homemade or canned chicken broth
2 sprigs Italian parsley
¼ teaspoon salt
Black pepper to taste
1 ripe, medium-size plantain, cut into
    ¼-inch-thick diagonal slices (optional)

PREPARATION

Heat 3 tablespoons oil in a large skillet over a medium flame. Add garlic and fideo and sauté for about 2 minutes, or until the fideo turns a golden brown. Using a blender, puree the tomato and onions until smooth. Add the pureed tomato sauce, chicken broth, parsley, salt, and pepper to the skillet. Cover and simmer for 5 minutes. (Add plantain slices about 5 minutes before serving, just enough to heat.) This is supposed to be a brothy soup; add more broth if needed. Serve immediately as the vermicelli will become soggy.

SERVES 4 TO 5

Fríjoles Refritos Estilo Guadalajara

Guadalajara-Style Refried Beans

1 tablespoon olive oil
1 dry Anaheim chile, washed, seeded, deveined
2 dry red *japonés* chiles, or 2 *chiles de árbol*, whole
¼ cup water
1 garlic clove
2 tablespoons finely chopped red onion
¼ cup chopped ripe tomato
2 cups whole cooked and drained pinto beans
   (reserve ¼ cup liquid)
Salt to taste

PREPARATION
Heat the oil in a large skillet over a medium flame. Sauté the Anaheim and *japonés* chiles for 30 seconds. Crush the chiles and oil from skillet in a *molcajete* or grind in a blender. Pour in bowl, and set aside.

In the same skillet, sauté the garlic, onions, and tomatoes for 2 minutes. Add to the blender and puree. Pour the pureed tomato and chile mixtures into the same hot skillet. The sauce should sizzle. Add the beans and heat thoroughly over a high flame. Mash the beans with a bean masher until they have a smooth consistency. Add the bean liquid, salt to taste, and stir. Simmer uncovered for about 10 minutes and serve hot. SERVES 4

Patas de Puerco Empanizados

Pigs' Feet in Egg Batter

1-½ quarts water
1 teaspoon salt
4 pigs' feet, cut in half and lengthwise
6 eggs, separated and at room temperature
2 tablespoons flour
½ cup flour
1 cup peanut oil

SAUCE
3 tablespoons olive oil
1 garlic clove, minced
1 small white onion, sliced thin
½ teaspoon dry whole Mexican oregano
½ teaspoon salt
3 tablespoons flour
1 cup roasted, peeled, seeded, and pureed
   tomato, or 1 cup canned tomato sauce
¼ cup chopped *cilantro*
4 cups chicken broth
Cilantro sprigs for garnish

Optional:
3 serrano chiles, roasted, seeded, and deveined
¼ cup water

PREPARATION

Into a large pot put 1-½ quarts water, 1 teaspoon salt, and pigs' feet. Cover and simmer for 1-½ hours. Remove the pigs' feet and cool.

Beat the egg whites in a bowl with wire whisk or pastry beater until firm peaks form. In another bowl, slightly beat the egg yolks, whisk in 2 tablespoons of flour, then fold into the egg whites with a spatula. Set aside.

Preheat oven to 200 degrees. Dredge pigs' feet in ½ cup flour and dip them in the beaten egg mixture until thoroughly coated. A thin coating is sufficient. Heat the peanut oil in a medium skillet over a medium-high flame. Sauté the pigs' feet until golden brown for about 1 minute on each side. Drain on paper towels. Keep warm in oven.

To make the sauce, heat 3 tablespoons of hot olive oil in a large skillet over a medium flame. Sauté garlic, onions, and oregano for 1 minute. Add salt and flour, stirring until flour becomes cream colored. Stir in tomatoes, *cilantro,* and broth. Cover and simmer for 15 minutes. (For a hotter sauce, grind 3 fire-roasted serrano chiles, seeded and deveined, and ¼ cup water. Add to the tomato sauce and simmer for 15 minutes.)

To serve, place the pig's feet on a large platter, and cover with the heated sauce. Garnish with whole *cilantro* sprigs. Serve as an entree with hot corn tortillas.

SERVES 4 TO 6

Guiso de Carne de Res con Ejotes

Steak and String Bean Stew

My father learned this recipe from Delfina. He usually made it when my mother worked nights. My sisters and I were rarely disappointed.

4 Anaheim chiles, roasted, sweated, peeled, seeded, deveined, and shredded into long strips
4 medium-size, ripe tomatoes, roasted, peeled, and pureed
4 tablespoons olive oil
1 small red onion, sliced thin
2 garlic cloves, minced
1 pound sirloin steak, cut into ½-inch-thick diagonal slices
1-½ cups water
½ pound green beans, trimmed, cut in half
1 teaspoon pepper
1 teaspoon salt
½ cup red wine

CONTINUED ON NEXT PAGE↪

PREPARATION

Fire-roast the Anaheim chiles and tomatoes over the stove burners until blistered and charred. Place chiles in a plastic bag and allow them to sweat in their own steam for 15 minutes. Peel the chiles, carefully removing as much charred skin as possible; remove seeds and stems. Shred the chiles into long strips. Peel off the charred skin from the roasted tomatoes and puree in a blender to a chunky texture.

In a large skillet, heat 2 tablespoons oil over a high flame. Sauté the meat, and set aside. In a large Dutch oven or heavy skillet, heat the remaining 2 tablespoons oil. Sauté the onions and garlic for 30 seconds. Add the steak, tomato puree, and water. Cover and simmer for 25 minutes. Uncover and add the string beans, Anaheim chiles, pepper, salt, and wine. Cover and continue simmering for another 10 minutes.

Serve with rice, hot crusty bread, or corn tortillas. SERVES 5

Chile de Árbol

Chile de Árbol

This recipe is for chile diehards: it's not a salad-like salsa for the timid. You can put it in a glass jar, cover it with a lid, and save it in the refrigerator for at least two months. It actually improves with aging, and it tastes better than any bottled chile sauce I know of.

1 ounce whole dry *chile de árbol*
1 tablespoon peanut oil
6 garlic cloves
3 teaspoons dry marjoram
10 whole black peppercorns
12 whole allspice
17 whole cloves
2 teaspoons salt
½ cup plain white vinegar
1 cup water

PREPARATION

Heat 1 tablespoon peanut oil in a small skillet over a medium flame. Sauté the chiles for about 30 seconds. Grind the chiles in a blender or food processor with garlic, marjoram, peppercorns, allspice, cloves, and salt for 3 minutes. Add vinegar and water and blend thoroughly. Serve in a glass or stainless-steel bowl, or store in a tightly covered glass jar and refrigerate.

MAKES ABOUT 2 CUPS OF CHILE SAUCE

After the Burn, the Glow

ONE MAY WONDER HOW SUCH A THOROUGHLY pugnacious fruit as chile ever became the world's most widely used condiment. With chiles such as the *habanero*, which is the most potent domesticated species on the market, how did the early Mesoamericans ever get it in their heads to bite this forbidding fruit, let alone develop a cuisine around it?

Plant chemists such as Dr. Eloy Rodriguez, the James Perkins Professor of Environmental Biology at Cornell University, is one of several scientists puzzled by this question. Although he has not come up with a definitive answer, Rodriguez said there's plenty of evidence to show that chiles indeed possess many admirable qualities, at least once you get past the immediate burning sensation.

So far, the more than 850 studies of chile's active chemical compounds indicate that chiles can help you lose weight, relieve joint pain, boost the circulatory system, and act as a powerful repellent against would-be muggers. When consumed in the fresh green form, this multitalented fruit contains twice as much vitamin C as oranges; when eaten in the dried form, it's an excellent source of vitamin A.

Still, chile has been blamed for such disorders as heartburn, indigestion, ulcers, and cancer. But experiments conducted at Baylor Medical School show that capsaicin, the active chemical agent in chile that tingles the tongue, is actually nonirritating. Capsaicin is also an antioxidant that retards the production of nitrosamines, which cause cancer. Other studies show that the use of chile has massive benefits to the heart as well as the arteries. Capsaicin reduces the number of blood clots in the blood vessels. It reduces blood pressure by causing the arteries to relax, and consequently strengthens the heartbeat. And there are benefits for both the weight-conscious and thrill seekers.

Regular consumers of chile benefit from an increase in their metabolic rate, thereby helping them reduce weight by burning carbohydrates more efficiently. The chile aficionado also knows that the initial burning sensation is followed by a numbing afterglow that allows the addict to increase the dosage and enter a new threshold of pleasure.

It is this unique numbing property that has made capsaicin the subject of intense research. For years, Native Americans have used chile for treating the pain of toothaches and childbirth. Recently, neurologists discovered that capsaicin effectively shuts down the nerves that transmit pain messages in conditions such as rheumatoid arthritis and phantom-limb pain.

Helado de Tuna

Prickly Pear Sorbet

Green, red, and purple-fleshed prickly pears, or the fruit of beavertail cactus, are sold in supermarkets throughout the Southwest and Mexican grocery stores nationwide. So you'll be surprised by the number of super- markets that sell this delicious fruit of the Opuntia species. Anyone living in the South- west should be able to scare up enough fruit from cacti grown in backyard gardens, or else purchase them from mail-order companies such as Frieda's.

6–7 pounds ripe prickly pears
½ cup light corn syrup
1 tablespoon fresh lime juice
2 tablespoons white tequila

STEP-BY-STEP PEN AND INK DRAWING
ILLUSTRATING METHOD FOR PEELING
A PRICKLY PEAR IN FOUR STEPS,
BY LUCENA VALLE

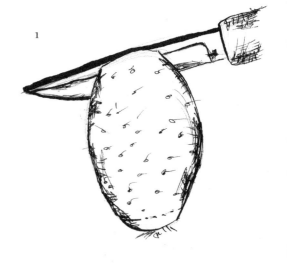

1

PREPARATION

Don a pair of rubber gloves before handling the prickly pears. Place them in a colander and rinse thoroughly while rubbing them gently. This will remove some of the little clusters of *aguates*, or fiberglass-like tufts of rudimentary spines called *glochidia*. They're very annoying if they get under our skin. They can be removed with fine tweezers or gum.

Cut a thin slice off the flower end and stem end of the pear at an angle perpendicular to the length of the fruit. Carefully make a series of shallow, lengthwise incisions into the pear's outer skin. Each cut should be about 2 inches apart. Slide the blade of a well-sharpened paring knife under each incision, running the blade lengthwise so as to separate the outer skin from the fruit. Repeat the procedure for each side of the incision until the skin just falls away in neat rectangles. Rinse the peeled fruit under cold water to remove any remaining *aguates*.

Place the peeled fruit in a blender and process to a smooth, watery consistency. Remove the seeds by straining the pureed fruit through a fine sieve directly into a large mixing bowl. The raw fruit produces 7 to 8 cups of strained juice. Whisk in the corn syrup, lime juice, and tequila, then pour into an ice cream maker and follow the manufacturer's directions.

SERVES 6

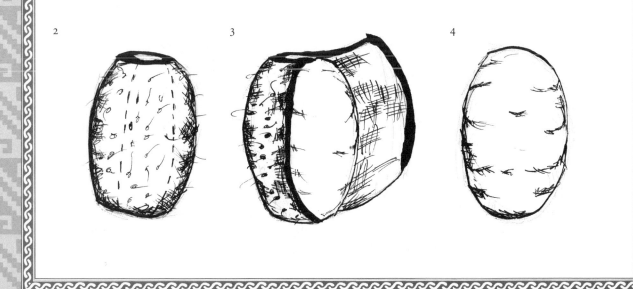

2   3   4

CHAPTER ELEVEN

the industrialization of mexican-american cuisine

VIRGINA FÁBREGAS, THE GREAT DAME OF Mexican theater touted on play-bills as "the pride of our race," dined with the members of her company at La Misión Café on Friday, May 13, 1927, the last night *Divorciémonos* (*Let's Divorce*) ran at the Capitol Theatre on Spring Street.

The Spanish-language newspaper *La Opinión* announced the event in a brief article appearing that day:

"Virgina Fábregas and her loyal collaborators shall be the toast of a simple dinner party offered by a group of her friends.

"Mrs. Bonzo, proprietress of the well-known La Misión Café, has been entrusted with preparing an exquisite dinner with which to honor the aforementioned persons. An orchestra shall enliven the genial gathering."

The story captures a moment in the resurgence of Mexican culture in Los Angeles. That year, despite low paid work, and the loneliness of exile, Mexicans now at least had enough spare time and spare change to enjoy something akin to the Harlem Renaissance, says social historian George F. Sanchez. This rebirth reflected the immigrant's cultural transformation. Paradoxically, Sanchez says, these strangers from different corners of Mexico now hungered for their roots, while searching for a new sense of community. Their search led them into the street, the square, the shops, and theaters, where they shared experiences of a popular culture that chronicled their struggles and adjustments to their new home.

By the time Delfina and her children arrived in Los Angeles, the resurgence of Mexican culture and cuisine was well underway.

In downtown bakeries, *tortillerías*, pool halls, dance halls, music halls, music stores, restaurants, bars, theaters, and even art galleries, the exiled immigrants found places where they could be Mexican in public.

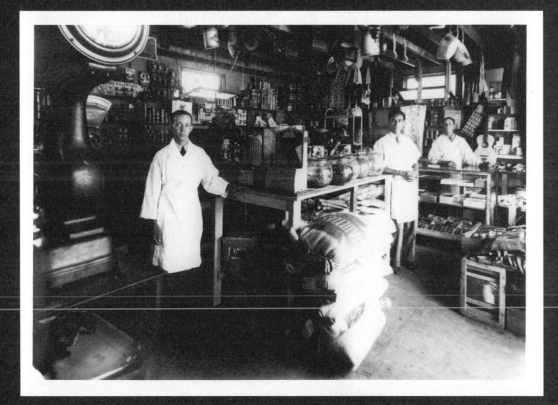

GROCERY STORE ON SOLANO AVENUE IN LOS ANGELES
OWNED BY AURELIO DOMINGUEZ,
ON LEFT, CIRCA 1925. *Courtesy Security Pacific Collection/L.A. Public Library*

The theaters, the most well-attended of these venues, were probably more popular than the churches, says Sanchez. At the time of the Fábregas performance, about a half-dozen downtown theaters regularly featured Spanish-language plays, musical revues, and silent movies, including Spanish-language films produced in Mexico. The late 1920s also marked a high point for Spanish-language theater in Los Angeles. Local and traveling companies performed works ranging from the sixteenth-century Spanish classics to crowd-pleasing potboilers. Catalina's brother, Carlos, wrote such a melodrama, *The Impunity of the Offense*, which was performed at the Mason Theatre. Estela and my father, about fourteen and eight respectively, saw the play, but only remember the audience's standing ovation, and their shouts of "Author! Author!" at the end of the play. No manuscript of the play survives, but Estela and her brother say it was about a bastard son who returns years later to find his father.

Just doors or streets away, a handful of music stores made records for local Mexican audiences. Various styles were performed, but the *corridos*, or story songs about the revolution they'd fled and the new country they'd found, were the most popular. A pair of these artists even had their own radio shows. Pedro J. Gonzalez, formerly Pancho Villa's telegraph operator, persuaded KMPC to give him his own early morning show, one of the country's first Spanish-language broadcasts. His program quickly attracted advertisers who recognized the Mexican community's growing purchasing power. Programs like Gonzalez's and newspapers like *La Opinión* provided information and entertainment that helped the Mexican community adapt to their new home while maintaining a link with the homeland. His group, Los Madrugadores, or Early Risers, performed his popular tune, *El Corrido del Lava-platos*, or the "Dishwasher's Ballad," a humorous account of Pedro's first working experiences upon crossing the border.

PHOTO OF CARLOS, CATALINA'S BROTHER, IN HIS EARLY 20S.

Often, after a night at the theater or after listening to Gonzalez's radio program, folks would treat themselves to meals in a restaurant like La Misión Café, which advertised "Exquisite Mexican Dishes." More than mere purveyors of food and drink, these establishments blurred the boundaries between private and public space, serving as living rooms for the homesick, archives of culinary memory, and a cozy place for politicos and business people to arrange their affairs.

Consuelo Bonzo, who founded La Misión in 1924, not only hired musicians and dancers to entertain her customers, she also invited the city's political leaders to communicate to them the concerns of the Mexican business community and hosted special celebrations such as the one for Virginia Fábregas. Consuelo also joined the *mutualista*, or mutual-aid groups that fed and clothed their indigent countrymen. Her political contacts paid off. After announcing its plans to demolish the businesses along Spring Street, the city offered Consuelo and her Italian husband, Alfredo, the old Pelanconi House, built around 1855, which was situated next to the old plaza in the middle of the new tourist destination called Olvera Street. They renamed their restaurant La Golondrina, after the sentimental farewell song, and Consuelo's mother, Refugio, developed the menu and ran the kitchen with Alfredo's help.

An early menu, which featured such items as chile con carne, enchiladas, chiles rellenos,

Golondrina and such, proclaimed La Golondrina the "VERY FIRSTMEXICAN RESTAURANT IN LOS ANGELES," which may have slightly exaggerated the truth. *La Crónica*, one of California's earliest Spanish-language newspapers, ran an ad for an eatery called El Cinco de Mayo, Fonda Mexicana, in an October 1877 edition.

At the turn of the century, there were few formal Mexican restaurants, and fewer yet that advertised in newspapers. Historian Antonio Rios-Bustamante suspects that a lot more selling

PHOTO OF A MIDDLE-AGED CARLOS IN
THEATRICAL GARB, PROBABLY TAKEN IN
LOS ANGELES IN THE 1920S.

of Mexican food occurred on street corners, under the canvas tarps of informal *tamaleros*, or in the boarding houses that catered to Mexican laborers. Before century's end, however, the marketing of Southern California real estate changed the meaning of its native cuisine. Charles Fletcher Lummis, the epitome of the booster journalist, and the *Los Angeles Times* publisher, Colonel Harrison Gray Otis, deserve much of the credit for reinventing the state's cultural legacy. Their partnership began September 12, 1884, after Lummis offered to walk from Cincinnati to Los Angeles, and write about his trek by installments for the *Times*. The colonel, who grasped the stunt's publicity potential, promised the native New Englander his paper's city editor's job if he kept his word. One hundred forty-three days later, the foot-sore Lummis trod into Los Angeles, and so forged the most dynamic publication relations partnership California had yet seen.

In no time, Lummis began to invent a new mythology for Southern California in newspaper articles, books, and magazine articles that combined sun worship and health faddism with nostalgia for bygone Spanish days. Lummis also reinvented himself.

Like other Eastern intellectuals of his generation, he'd become disillusioned with the ideals of American democracy; the capitalist robber barons didn't need reform-minded do-gooders and middle-class self-improvers to run the Republican party. Feeling left out, as well as disgusted by the greed of monopoly capitalism exposed by the muckrakers, he and other disenchanted intellectuals searched for a new homeland. They found it in California and the greater Southwest, a landscape they imagined as "enchanting" rather than simply savage. Refashioning the past to their personal advantage, they now saw themselves husbanding a fallen Hispanic civilization.

Lummis, for his part, assumed the pose of a Spanish grandee, going so far as to call himself Don Carlos, a conceit, writes historian James W. Byrkit, that evokes the imagery of the Southern Lost Cause: "Indians toil happily in the fields for Padre Agustín or Don José, rather than blacks for Ol' Massa; *caballero* is just another name for cavalier; sprawling ranchos...replace the colonnaded mansions." Both mythologies, Byrkit adds, glorify the "loftier aspects of Western civilization: traditions, leisure, refined literary tastes, sartorial formality, and well-bred social graces, including courtliness."

And what better symbol of loftiness than California's abandoned missions, since crumbling adobe could evoke a time when gentle padres presided over vast pastoral domains. Lummis understood the myth's bankability, writing that "the Missions are, next to our climate and its consequences, the best capital Southern California has."

This pleased his boss at the *Los Angeles Times*. Otis, who harbored insecurities about Southern California's image as a cultural wasteland good only for convalescing tuberculars, endorsed Lummis's patrician myth, but suppressed the fact that the Franciscans had flogged runaway Indians, or that Yankee freebooters lynched and swindled California's Spanish and Mexican settlers. Lummis wanted to reassure the affluent Babbitry of the Middle West, so sought after by Otis as real estate investors, that Los Angeles offered them a Spanish-flavored European refinement. And anything, including cookbooks, could be made into symbols of bourgeois gentility.

While writing books and editing the *Times*, Lummis developed a fondness for Mexican food and built a Spanish-style home just north of Los Angeles on the banks of the creek bed called *Arroyo Seco*. He dubbed it *El Alisal*, "the place of the Sycamores," a stage where he held court, entertaining artists and intellectuals with dinner parties that featured Mexican cooking. With support of members such as Colonel Harrison Gray Otis, Lummis also founded the Landmarks Club, a group that worked to preserve the missions from further decay.

IN 1903, THE LANDMARKS CLUB PUBLISHED *THE Landmarks Club Cook Book* to finance its preservation efforts. Lummis, the club's president, wrote the foreward to one of the first English-language cookbooks to dedicate a section to "old Californian and Mexican dishes." This cookbook steeped in mission imagery provided more than financing for the club's preservation efforts. Lummis embraced Mexican cuisine only to frame its Mexican origins within what he perceived as a more romantic Spanish, more European, legacy.

Soon after, cookbook writers and restaurant owners swept up in Lummis's Mission Revival movement also made their enchiladas and tamales more palatable for non-Mexican diners by calling them "authentic" Spanish cuisine. The Spanish Kitchen, located at 127 North Broadway,

in the heart of downtown, advertised to English-language readers its "Beef & Chicken Tamales" in the March 16, 1912 edition of the *Los Angeles Record*. The restaurant was run by Ismael Ramirez, who was also said to be popular with theater people. The restaurant ad promised, "The only place in the city where you can get a genuine Spanish Dinner," followed by a rather un-Spanish-sounding list of dishes: "Special Chicken Tamales/Spanish Tamales/Enchiladas/Spanish Beans/Tortillas." Other restaurants offered similar fare.

The 1914 edition of Bertha Haffner Ginger's *California Mexican-Spanish Cook Book* offers a "Regular Spanish Dinner" lifted from an unnamed restaurant. The menu consisted of "Soup/Salad/Enchiladas/Carne con Chili/Spanish Beans/Spanish Rice/Fruit and Coffee." The repetition of entrees like enchiladas, chile con carne, tamales, and so forth, signaled the appearance of a standardized cuisine that would, until very recently, dominate the menus of most Mexican-American restaurants.

Inventing a
Fantasy Cuisine

You might say that cookbook writer Bertha Haffner Ginger was an heir of Charles Fletcher Lummis and Colonel Harrison Gray Otis. In addition to compiling a cookbook filled with atrocious Spanish spellings and mediocre recipes, Ginger's *California Mexican-Spanish Cook Book* perpetuated key elements of the Hispanicized mythology Lummis and Otis invented for California.

Ginger, however, did try to set the record straight. In the book's introduction, she wrote: "It is not generally known that Spanish as they are known in California are really Mexican dishes. Bread made of corn, sauces of chile peppers, jerked beef, tortillas, enchiladas, etc., are unknown in Spain as native foods . . ." She just didn't follow through. She instead rationalized the cuisine's misrepresentation by asserting that since the "majority of Spanish people in California are as devoted to peppery dishes as the Mexicans themselves, and as the Mexicans speak Spanish, the foods are commonly called Spanish dishes."

Was Ginger too naive to detect the illogic of what she'd proposed, or was hers an ignorance of convenience? It would have been far more honest to write that the term "Spanish food" simply did not apply, and leave it at that. But I suspect that Ginger knew that such honesty would put her at odds with the prevailing mythology fostered by Lummis and friends. So she played along.

Ginger's book invoked Lummis's Mission Revival myth by including so-called Regular Spanish Dinner menus, photos of "Spanish" señoritas, and a photo of the dome-shaped oven next to which Ramona, the tragic Indian protaganist of Helen Hunt Jackson's 1884 novel by the same name, was allegedly married. Although the muckraking novel condemned the abuse of California Indians, Los Angeles chronicler Mike Davis writes that Lummis and Otis had drained the novel of its politics to sell real estate and lead mission-themed pageants to distract rebellious Los Angeles workers.

A decade later, Ginger used the Ramona myth to help package her book. After all, she, like so many others, couldn't deny her audience a taste of the romance that had lured them to California in the first place.

And the myth would live on more than a half century longer in California's "Spanish" restaurants and mission cookbooks that dreamed of "dark-eyed señoritas with roses held between their teeth as they danced the *jota*.

PARADOXICALLY, AT THE MOMENT MEXICAN-American cuisine took the form we recognize today, the yearly arrival of thousands of Mexicans acted as a catalyst that instigated a demand for more authentic cuisine, not the standard rice-bean-and-enchilada platter. New restaurants opened, menus became more elaborate, and restaurant owners tried to cash in on nationalist sympathies by running ads during Mexican national and religious holidays promising "authentic" Mexican fare.

In 1921, two days before the sixteenth of September, the holiday celebrating Mexico's independence from Spain, the Gran Restaurant Mexico offered "one of those Xochimilco meals that shall remind of better days back home." The menu listed "real mole poblano," enchiladas with cream, fried chicken, breaded pigs' feet, atole with milk, *champurrado* with *piloncillo,* tostadas with meat and vegetables, chile with melted cheese, refried beans, *chalupitas* filled with meat and potatoes, chile verde stew, and huevos rancheros. The Sanroman Restaurant offered such authentic-sounding entrees as barbequed lamb's heads, turkey mole, chicken in *pipian,* a pumpkin seed–based mole, and *nopalitos,* or fresh cactus. It's impossible to tell from the ads just how "authentic" the cooking was, but it clearly catered to a working-class immigrant clientele, many of whom lived in nearby boardinghouses.

In 1923, Rosa Moreno and Alejandro Borquez opened what they claimed was the city's other "first Mexican restaurant" near the Memorial Coliseum, then at the city's southwestern edge. The restaurant's distance from the city's Mexican core,

which was farther to the east, meant that Alejandro and Rosa served a mixed clientele of Mexicans and Anglos, including risen stars like Harold Lloyd, or rising ones like Gary Cooper. Their Sonora Café, later named El Cholo in 1927, offered a menu that reflected their dual audience, and so represented the next stage in the evolution of what some call "Calmex" cuisine.

An early restaurant menu, most of it in English, lists a sixty-cent combination plate with the following items:

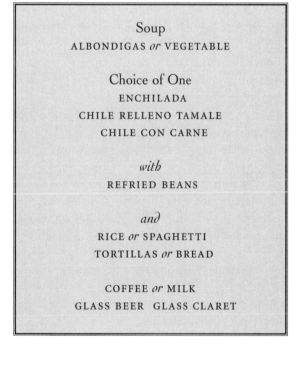

Soup
ALBONDIGAS *or* VEGETABLE

Choice of One
ENCHILADA
CHILE RELLENO TAMALE
CHILE CON CARNE

with
REFRIED BEANS

and
RICE *or* SPAGHETTI
TORTILLAS *or* BREAD

COFFEE *or* MILK
GLASS BEER   GLASS CLARET

AT A LINGUISTIC LEVEL, THE BILINGUALISM OF the combination-plate menu suggests an accommodation in which Spanish is given a status equal to English. But a closer look reveals this to be untrue. Rosa and Alejandro's daughter, Aurelia, points out that dishes were often renamed. Spaghetti, for example, was really *Sopa de fideos*, or lightly toasted vermicelli pasta, which Rosa simmered in a beef broth, Sonora-style. At a culinary level, the menu effectively reduced a whole cuisine into a few combination plates. Such extreme oversimplification reflected the diner's ignorance, or lack of culinary curiosity. Like a mirror, the menus of restaurants similar to the Sonora Café show their customers to be tourist diners who lacked the knowledge to demand authenticity; for them a familiar deviation from the daily routine was exotic enough.

The first efforts to mass-produce Mexican food exacerbated the problem. Gradually, as Mexican food made its way from the restaurant to the factory, elaborate recipes were sacrificed to the gods of industrial efficiency. By the 1920s, the industrialization of food manufacturing was well under way, as evidenced by such innovations as standardized packaging, national merchandising, and identifiable trademarks. Slowly, Mexican food manufacturers and restaurant owners began to adopt the new industrial rationale, and so lay the foundation for mass marketing Mexican-American cuisine, the product of a technological *mestizaje*. In time, the invention of a "Spanish fantasy" cuisine (to borrow a phrase from Carey McWilliams), compromises to Anglo taste, and the demands of mass production combined to create the stereotypical heated combination plate loaded with Spanish rice, refried beans, and red enchilida coated with Day-Glo cheddar.

Fortunately, Delfina did not earn enough to treat her children to the Mexican-American food served at these "Spanish" restaurants. Like so many of her countrymen, she could not afford to be distracted from her inevitable moments of homesickness and loneliness—hardships that sharpened the tastes of her memories.

between two worlds

BY THE WINTER OF 1930, LOS ANGELES WAS deep in the Depression. The seamstress jobs Delfina got in the garment district that had allowed her to leave the Roger Jessup dairy and rent a flimsy two-bedroom house on Hunter Street in East Los Angeles had become scarce. The newspaper and radio reports that began the winter of 1931 only added to her worries.

On February 26, immigration agents and local police closed off the downtown plaza's exits before interrogating about four hundred people who had gathered there to sit in the sun and chat with friends. The plaza was raided for symbolic reasons. Despite past efforts of groups such as Charles Fletcher Lummis's Landmarks Club to "preserve" the plaza for tourism, it had again become a gathering place for Mexicans. They returned to the heart of the city to discuss politics, reminisce about home, shop at the surrounding stores, or attend the theater. Going to the plaza became one more gesture with which Mexicans publicly remembered that California had once belonged to them. It mattered little if the authorities released the eleven Mexicans they had apprehended. Their claim to a legitimate and public place in Los Angeles had been challenged. The Hoover administration, together with members of the Los Angeles Chamber of Commerce, targeted the Mexicans as scapegoats. They blamed the economic havoc created by the Depression on "alien" labor "radicals."

More than three million suspected union troublemakers had been similarly ejected during the previous decade. This time Mexicans, especially those joining unions, became prime targets of "Operation Wetback," a quasi-official campaign designed to take jobs held by Mexicans and give them to unemployed "Americans." That the Mexicans had no jobs to give up didn't seem to matter.

The local newspapers, also chamber members, played a crucial role in the campaign. They heightened the "repatriation" terror to which an isolated and homesick Mexican community was especially vulnerable. Even after Roosevelt entered office, and ended federal involvement in "Operation Wetback," chamber members pressed hard to maintain the illusion of an official campaign to bribe or bully Mexicans into leaving. One-way train tickets paid for with county funds were freely distributed to families who were cut off county relief, farm land in Mexico was promised; anything, in other words, to induce them to leave quietly.

In the city that manufactured dreams, the campaign signaled a public relations milestone: the Chamber of Commerce, through its member newspapers and public relations operatives, succeeded in making the word "alien" synonymous with Mexican so as to justify the suspension of their civil rights. The deep-rooted historical claim Mexicans made to the Southwest, both as its earliest, founding citizens, and then later, as the work force that built its industries, counted for nothing. A decade later, the same public relations machine would be turned against American citizens of Japanese ancestry.

Some, like Delfina, qualified for legal residency. But like thousands of other Mexicans, she remained ignorant of her residency rights. Local media and local government misinformation, confusing immigration laws published in English, as well as the immigrants' mistrust of official government, discouraged them from exercising their rights. So, as the hysteria mounted and the Depression deepened, tens of thousands of Mexicans gave up, believing they'd ever become equal to gringo citizens. For the children of immigrants who had grown attached to their new home, repatriation was a crushing betrayal.

About all they could count on from their newly adopted country was train fare and some pocket money. So the immigrants thus turned inward, to one another. Only family loyalties mattered. More than 400,000 were tricked, bullied, or bribed into leaving. Those who stayed behind learned a different lesson: Anglo indifference became blatant, virulent racism, which left its own lasting scars.

Then, in 1931, in the midst of the deepening fear, Delfina received another letter. Her aunt Trinidad wrote to Delfina, saying that her husband was gravely ill, that he'd lost everything, that he was now alone, and certain to die in misery. Trinidad's letter came gilded in guilt. Shouldn't the children return the Guadalajara to see their father one last time? Trinidad also implied that Delfina had overreacted to her husband's indiscretions, that she should have returned three years ago to defend her place at his side. Delfina, partly out of loyalty to Catalina, who educated her, couldn't ignore her aunt's request. And so she decided to follow the thousands who submitted to "voluntary repatriation." The family now consisted of Delfina and her sons, including my father, Manuel. Estela, who had recently married, decided to take her chances and stay in Los Angeles with her husband, Julio.

My father's first impression upon arriving in Guadalajara was how old and small it seemed compared to Los Angeles, where he remembered the buildings tall and new, the streets clean and wide. Most of all, he missed the Red Car, the legendary rail system that made sprawling Los Angeles manageable, even for a fifth grader. He was also frustrated. "I was just beginning to get the hang of it in school," when he had to change countries again.

During the brief time they were reacquainted, my father distinctly remembers mealtimes, particularly when he was sent, pot in hand, to the church soup line, where he waited to receive the only meal his family would eat that day. He usually returned with a *puchero* of mostly vegetables. His mother served the children first, then herself. His father served himself last, taking whatever was left after the children had eaten. Usually there was little left. As Pablo's health deteriorated, my father recalls how, even near death, he maintained a nearly imperturbable patience and affection for his family—until the day he died.

Delfina buried Pablo and continued sewing men's overalls to earn money. My father, then about nine years old, ran errands as a delivery boy for a pair of eccentric old sisters who ran a perfume store. They gave this scrawny kid a buffalo of a bicycle. In a heavy wrought-iron basket big enough to carry an infant above the bike's front balloon tire, he conveyed tiny tinkling bottles of scented essences over cobblestoned streets, through blind intersections, to clients who rarely paid. They also sent him to the distillery. The pair of proper spinsters specified *Herradura*, the cognac of agave spirits known for its horseshoe trademark. They, in turn, taught my dad to sip tequila like a man—first a bite of lemon, then a lick of salt, followed by a sweet perfumed sip of fire.

Difficult years followed for the repatriated.

Thrown back into the precarious conditions they'd tried to escape a decade before, they were forced to rely on skills learned *en el otro lado*. Eventually, after many tries, most, including Delfina and her sons, returned to the United States. But they did not return with the enthusiasm of their first crossing. After all, both countries—the impoverished Mexico they left, and the United States which they had learned to love—had betrayed them. And they were not going to raise their hopes in a country that had deported them.

Several years after returning to Southern California, my father met and married my mother before the outbreak of World War II. But this was not his last return. Several months after the country plunged into war, my father did something he would regret for years afterward. He dodged the draft, stepping across the border at Tijuana with my mother, Lilly. No doubt his decision saved him from the death or maiming that awaited a disproportionately high number of Mexican enlisted men. But escaping to Tijuana made him a fugitive for almost a half century. He accepted his exile with few complaints, an episode that belongs to another story.

on the border

GIVEN THEIR LIMITED options, Tijuana was about the best place my parents could choose to wait out the War. It was as close as they could get to their families, including Delfina, who had settled near Los Angeles.

More importantly, the flow of dollars made Tijuana an unofficial appendage of the United States economy, which had clear advantages. As far as Mexican cities went, Tijuana's residents earned among the highest standards of living, even after the war-related jobs in San Diego disappeared along with the Mexican government's ban against gambling. It had grown as a bastard city, needed by both countries for its cross-border commerce and vices, but basically orphaned by Mexico City and Washington. At the time, gambling and prostitution were giving way to the peacetime business of servicing a city approaching fifty thousand, and twice as many weekend tourists. Its hillsides and dusty canyons were not yet fully encrusted with flimsy shacks, nor its garbage dump yet rich enough to feed a city of trash pickers.

Tijuana grew between frontiers. To the north stretched a border of desire and fear; to the south, Baja's skinny leg of rugged mountains, desolate beaches, exotic thorn forests, failed utopias, abandoned mining camps. Tijuana buttoned these frontiers together in a place where the newcomers dreamed of dollars. Each day they arrived—desperate, ambitious immigrants from western Mexico, rising and falling movie stars, outlaws and hustlers of every nationality.

MY PARENTS, LILLY AND VICTOR MANUEL VALLE, ON THEIR WEDDING DAY

Like my parents, people came to start over, to escape, to forget, to take chances. During the time they lived in Tijuana, my parents tried their hands at several businesses. But they got their best results from the *tortillería* they started in 1945, which they ran inside the hulking block of a grocery store called El Adobe. In no time, their enterprise earned a reputation for quality.

"Our tortillas were famous in Tijuana," my mother, Lilly, said. "The restaurants, the doctors, all the people who had professions, would send their maids to stand in line" for the thinnest, most supple handmade corn tortillas in town.

Of course, running a *tortillería* in a cramped workroom behind the store was a matter of survival for my parents. For a time, it gave them an honest, though precarious, livelihood. And it had other benefits.

Tijuana baptised my mother into adulthood. She learned that the world was unjust, especially to the poor, and that Mexico's heart beat there as strongly as in any other city of the interior. Together, in their newly adopted city, my parents reinvented a cuisine, discovered Baja's seafood, and learned more than they'd expected to about tortillas and the people who made them.

They also struggled with a stubborn irony: Though indigenous farmers began to cultivate wild maize almost ten thousand years ago, during and after the war years Mexico had come to depend upon a steady flow of grain imported from the midwestern United States. Tijuana got very little of this grain since most of it was shipped to the Mexican interior. Washed-out roads, red tape at the border, peso devaluations, or droughts could also spell the difference between great, lousy, or no tortillas at all.

Bad grain made the *tortilleras* grumble and curse as they struggled to make their tortillas hold together. Corn grown on Sonora's dry mountainsides produced grain so hard it overheated and gummed up the millstones. My father then had to switch off the mill's gas-powered motor, remove and clean its fifty-pound black basalt discs, and rechisel the grinding grooves that radiated outward in whorls.

When the grain was good, the *tortilleras* purred. The high oil content of premium grain gave the *masa* elasticity. In a flutter of palms, they clapped out thin moons that rose from the griddle supple enough to pass the crucial test—it could be rolled into a tightly wrapped taco in a single motion by sliding the heel of the palm over an outstretched tortilla held on the other hand. When the grain was good, and the mornings cold, the *tortilleras* silenced their bellies with *gorditas de manteca*, thick palm-size tortillas packed with crumbled raw sugar and whole anise seed, or crumbly *cotija* cheese, and sizzled in fat till golden, then swallowed in cautious bites between near-scalding slurps of coffee laced with cinnamon, raw sugar, and a shot of tequila that tickled the nose with elusive vapors. Of such mornings my mother remembers the sounds:

Wet stone against wet stone, back-forth, back-forth in quick muffled strokes over the *metates*—clap clap clap—grinding the *masa* even finer—clap clap—sprinkled water droplets skittering off the table-length griddle—clap clap clap—followed by laughter—clap clap—quick hisses of tortillas hitting the griddle—clap clap—voices counting tortillas out loud—clap clap clap—as they pile up, steaming, fragrant of toasted corn.

In the midst of these sounds and flavors, the *tortilleras* gossiped and talked, revealing themselves in their stories and the tortillas they made. Estefa, for example, "would always leave a small lump in the middle of her tortillas," my mother said. "They were very thin, but always with a lump in the middle. We would tell her not to do that, but they always came out the same way."

Though their clientele loved hand-patted tortillas, they nevertheless shunned the women who left their palm prints on their tortillas. Even in Tijuana, a town far from older class-conscious Mexican cities, *tortilleras* occupied the bottom social rungs. Though they preserved the knowledge of their Mesoamerican ancestors in the table's daily pillar of tortillas, to call someone a *tortillera* was to accuse that person of passivity, Indian backwardness, and poverty. My mother knew only the last of the insults to be true.

Each day she drove the *tortilleras* home to their shacks that clung to mangy hillsides at precarious random angles. In summer, the *tortilleras* and their families shared the ever-present dust with the ever-biting fleas. Sewage cut ruts down paths that passed for streets. During the rainy months, the "streets" became mud rivers, hillsides slid, collapsing shacks like faded playing cards. Yet my mother identified with the *tortilleras* because of their pride, their uncompromising work ethic, and because they adopted her—a Chicana born and raised near Los Angeles—as a daughter. By

contrast, the so-called *gente decente* (the decent folks) rarely passed up opportunities to correct her imperfect Spanish, their way of reminding my mother she was an outsider—*una Americana*—out of place in Tijuana.

To assist them and make sure their business got off the ground, Delfina left Canta Ranas, her barrio in southeast Los Angeles, where she lived with her daughter, Estela. Besides sorting vegetables and dusting tin cans, Delfina spent some cooking time with my mother, introducing her to such classic Jalisco dishes as *Tacos de crema*, helped with the brandy-cured *longaniza* sausage my dad made for the store, or *flautas*, deep-fried, tightly rolled tacos filled with shredded flank steak dipped in guacamole textured with jewel-like pomegranate seeds. To my mother, whose home cooking typified her family's Chihuahuan appetite for beef, flour tortillas, and chile, Delfina's cooking was both a challenge and a revelation.

"She [Delfina] was a superb cook," my mother said. "If she taught anyone, she wanted them to learn to do things her way. Like the *recaudo* [a puree of roasted tomato with onion or garlic added to soups or sauces], which is a basic part of Mexican food. To me, some of these things seemed like minor details. But she would get angry if you didn't do it her way."

Despite Delfina's help, their profitable *tortillería*, and income earned from El Adobe's grocery store and butcher shop, the business could not quite cover the debts they'd assumed from their partners. So they had to find ways to cut costs and increase profits. That's when their adventures began.

On Sundays, the one day they didn't make tortillas, my parents closed the Adobe to drive out into the surrounding country to buy merchandise directly from the farmers at a lower cost. With my eldest sister, Otila, snug in her basket in the bed of their Model A truck, my parents forded swollen creeks, clambered up rocky trails that disappeared into mountainsides, and raced over sandy river bottoms, all before four-wheel-drive RVs.

From local farmers they bought *hojas*, the dried leaves from ears of corn for wrapping tamales, hard wheels of salty cheese, sacks of beans or sweet corn, the garland-like *ristras* of dried chile, or a live hog, when they could. Anything, so long as they could sell it or eat it themselves, and drive back with a story to tell. Like the time they drove out to a ranch expecting to do business, but were instead invited to a wedding banquet, and so saved the risks of a long drive back on darkened roads.

"'Come on in, come on in,'" my mother remembers her host's invitation.

"'Well, we came to do some business,'" she answered.

"'What business? Come on in and dance.' So we danced while they took care of the baby. Oh, they were nice people." Their hosts fed them, gave them a room for the night, and breakfast the next morning, never expecting repayment.

Other times, they sipped wines in Santa Tomas, tasted briny olives near Mañadero, slurped down huge, sweet raw clams squirted with lime juice and bottled chile in Ensenada; slowly savored the broth of a *cahuama*, green sea turtle simmered in copious quantities of red wine, herbs, and aromatic vegetables, a delicacy of Babbette-like proportions prepared outdoors in front of a raunchy Tijuana cantina.

They even descended cliffs as steep and majestic as Big Sur's for a bowl of soup. Juan and Berta Ulloa, owners of a secondhand store across from El Adobe, invited my parents to their ranch: a few green pastures suspended between rocky cliffs and crashing surf. The ranch north of Ensenada seemed a self-sufficient world. Above their homestead, in terraced fields, they grew beans and wheat and raised a few cattle. By the house, from the cliff face, trickled a spring that collected in a jade pond flecked with tiny fin flashes. Below, from a sheltering cove, Juan and sons rowed a boat out far enough to fish or dive for abalone. That night Berta served a soup improvised from their garden vegetables, fresh oregano, and hefty abalone pried from rocks, then pounded for the pot. Nothing fancy, not for such a delicacy as abalone; quickly simmered, its broth was tangy, sweet, and faintly tasting of kelp carried in the breeze. They didn't know overharvesting of the narrow litoral ribbon stretching from Baja to Alaska might some day make abalone an almost forbidden pleasure.

MY PARENTS STUCK WITH EL ADOBE AS BEST THEY could until peso devaluations, a robbery, and debts forced them to consider selling.

During the decade they had lived in Tijuana, they had survived by saying yes to nearly every opportunity that came along. They ran a dry cleaners, until they went broke paying for a

THE SCRAPWOOD HOUSE BUILT NEAR THE TIJUANA RIVER.
ABOUT A DOZEN RELATIVES WITH MY GRANDMOTHER
DELFINA ON THE FAR LEFT, CIRCA 1949.

suede coat they ruined, operated a dairy of five cows, until the herd died of indigestion from grazing on tender grass, and ran a dance hall that swayed when people danced, until local gangsters demanded protection money. Now they faced the inevitable. Soon, they'd have to sell their business, vacate the living quarters they rented behind the Adobe, and look for jobs selling curios to the tourists.

But not just yet. My parents still had time to scheme. My father learned from a Lieutenant España in the Mexican army that he could get a patch of land upon which to build a house, grow crops, raise some pigs, and not pay a single centavo in rent. The first step required applying to the federal government for a vacant parcel on the flood plane of the Tijuana River. They got a piece, three decades before the government cleared out squatters for a trendy shopping mall, mega-discos, and a state-run Casa Cultural where tourists could see the "wonders" of Mexico. My father quickly bought a gas-powered pump to irrigate about a dozen acres of silty riverbed, on which he planted corn, tomatoes, and radishes he sold in the Adobe. In the meantime, he designed a house with the basic drafting skills he had picked up in school and scrounged up disassembled house-sized wooden crates in which the United States government shipped heavy military supplies. The sides of the crates—thick boards framed with 2 x 4s—made ready walls. All he had to do was saw out doors and windows.

With the help of a carpenter friend, my parents erected a three-bedroom wood-framed house, which they placed atop three-foot footings as a protection from flooding. It even had a porch with a view of the river, dusty and dry as it usually was, and the Caliente Racetrack in the distance. Quite a pastoral dream come true for my father. He'd always wanted his own farm, and now he had one just blocks from downtown Tijuana. That's when the *"ejército"* came, just before he put on the finishing touches.

One afternoon, as my parents walked toward the house to resume work, four Mexican soldiers stopped them. They told them that it was against the law to build a house on federal land; anyway, the river was bound to wash it away. Just like today, houses, people, cars, and cows were swept away with a heavy rain, flushing bloated corpses of squatters and livestock out to the Pacific. Again, my father turned to his advisor on military matters. Lieutenant España told him the soldiers could not dislodge them once they'd moved into the house. So my parents planned to wait, then rush in with their few belongings the moment the soldiers went on patrol.

For a few days they spied, memorizing the soldiers' daily routine. Then they made their move on a drizzling afternoon. They had loaded up their truck and a friend's Buick with belongings and headed toward the riverbed. The first run went smoothly. But on the second trip, the cars sunk into the river silt a short distance from their house. Far off in the distance, they saw the soldiers returning. My mother, who was pregnant, said she became frightened for the first time. What if they were caught with half their belongings inside the house, the rest of it getting wet in the rain? They had no choice but to unload where they were, then frantically dig to free their wheels from the slop. Fortunately, they snuck in just before the soldiers arrived.

Like the wolf in the fairy tale, the soldiers came to their door several times. Sometimes, they turned up when my mom was alone with my two eldest sisters. They announced their arrival, pounding the door with rifle butts, shouting, "'*Quién vive aquí*? Who lives here?'"

"I would say, 'It's us, it's us.'"

"Then they'd order, '*Sálganse*. Come out! Come out!'"

"And I would say, 'No! We're not coming out, we're not coming out.' I wasn't a bit afraid," my mother said.

She turned the soldiers back several times, even though they could have forced their way in if they had wanted to. They either lacked the authority to do so, or my mom and my sisters reminded them of their own families, squatting on someone else's land. My parents think back now at what they did and laugh. They were so cocky, so cunning. "I think other people would've given up from all the things we did," my mother says. "Your father never gave up."

"I couldn't," my father said. "I had to feed a family. There was no way out. Like the saying goes: 'It's the shoe's tightness that makes you walk.'"

They also laugh at their big dreams and their modest means. My father built the house in the image of the proper suburban homes he'd admired as a kid in Los Angeles, but the incongruity of what and where he built it reminded him of a scene from Charlie Chaplin's *Modern Times*, his favorite movie. In a parody of suburban paradise, the tramp and his sweetheart play house in a shack near a stream that looks deep, but is actually inches shallow. For a moment, they pretend to live happily-ever-after until Chaplin steps through the shack's rotten floor, and a factory whistle reminds him that he's unemployed and his stomach is growling.

My parents came to a similar realization. No matter how many trinkets they sold to the tourists, or how long they ignored the river, they knew that they would never earn enough to satisfy needs they had dreamed in another landscape; that their residence on the river was temporary. So it was time to try again.

They made their escape in stages. First my mom, the citizen, crossed the border in her last hours of pregnancy, squeezing her legs together to hold me in long enough to get to the hospital in Fullerton, California, where I was born on November 10, 1950. On the way there, she remembers her sister driving through orchards. Between the rows she saw avocados a furious Santa Ana had blown to the ground. A few days later she returned with me to Tijuana to help my father plan phase two of their escape.

Weeks later, she walked past the American border guards without difficulty since she was a United States citizen. She stopped within viewing distance of the border, and waited. My father, no longer a citizen, had to be devious. He sauntered up to the border gate wearing a flashy silk print shirt, pressed baggy slacks cinched high at the waist, holding a small bottle of tequila, betting the border guards would take him for an Americano. But the guards stopped him.

"Hey, buddy, you can't do that."

"What?" my father asked.

"Cross with tequila. You'll have to go back or leave it."

"No, I won't," my father said. "I'll drink it right here," which he did, guzzling it down in front of them. The guards were so baffled by the display they didn't think to stop him. As he walked by, he felt the buzz of the liquor going to his head, the terrifying anxiety of expecting a tap on his shoulder, and the thrill of having fooled the *migra* (border patrol) that day in late December.

In the years that followed, they raised four kids in Southern California's suburbs, sent them to college, built up a jewelry business, married kids off, protested wars, boycotted grapes, and defended undocumented Latino workers. All the while, my dad lived the life of a spy who had burrowed so deep underground that he sometimes forgot why he'd forfeited his citizenship.

When my parents retired, they owned a cabin in the mountains and the kind of two-story Victorian wood-framed house my father had so admired as a kid in Los Angeles. Nothing lavish, just comfortably cozy, and within walking distance of daughters, nephews, nieces, and great-grandchildren. My father satisfied another whim: he restored a 1931 Chevrolet Cabriolet to mint condition. Factory paint, original engine, everything. It took forever, but he finally did it, reclaiming a piece of the childhood he'd left behind in Los Angeles in 1931.

My parents sometimes drove the car in patriotic parades. The funny thing was, my dad was an "illegal" when he drove it past city fathers and mildly amused crowds. He'd eluded citizenship, Ping-Ponging across the border in retreats and escapes too complicated to retell. Needless to say, my father's experience altered his perception of life north and south of the border. The rich and the "illegals" know how the world really works; factories need cheap labor, Hollywood producers need nannies and cooks; the poor need to work to survive. When you play by these rules, getting across doubles as a moral victory and an economic defeat, or vice versa.

My dad survived the rules. On June 15, 1989, he pulled his green card out of the mailbox. And he knew exactly what he wanted to do with it. Thirty-nine years after leaving Tijuana without expecting to return, he drove my mom past the border guards in a Winnebago. They go back to Baja now and then. The fishing, my dad says; the God-fearing people, my mom says. I think they see themselves in the youthful faces of those waiting to cross over. My father has his own reasons for returning. It's his way of accepting his failures, and his betrayals. Having learned the hard lessons of losing the country of his birth, and the country of his choosing, he now vows his allegiance to both.

Ceviche de Abulón

Abalone Ceviche

The perfect summertime meal. My mom made this when it was just too hot to cook. No cooking involved, just chopping, squeezing, and can opening.

1-½ cups canned, diced abalone or conch (reserve liquid)
¼ cup canned, sliced serrano chiles in *escabeche*, drained (reserve 3 tablespoons liquid)
4 whole green onions, chopped fine
½ medium white onion, chopped fine
¾ cup Italian parsley, chopped fine
½ cucumber, peeled and chopped
1 large ripe tomato, chopped
2 teaspoons fresh lime juice
Salt and black pepper to taste
Lemon wedges

PREPARATION
Combine ingredients in a large bowl. Cover and marinate for 4 hours. Serve on a bed of lettuce in a large bowl with crackers or tortilla chips. Garnish with lemon wedges.
SERVES 4

Puchero de Pescado

Mexican Cod Chowder

It may seem odd, but hot soup on a hot day can be very refreshing. The strained stock from this recipe makes an excellent fumet.

2 ripe tomatoes, chopped
1 medium yellow onion, quartered
3 garlic cloves
3 tablespoons extra virgin olive oil
1 tablespoon dried whole Mexican oregano
1 bay leaf
8 cups hot water
1-½ pounds halibut, cod, or other firm-fleshed fillets, cut into 2" x 2" squares
4 small red potatoes, peeled and chopped
2 medium carrots, peeled and chopped
3 yellow squash, chopped
1 cup coarsely chopped string beans
10 green stuffed olives
1 pickled jalapeño chile, cut lengthwise
1 teaspoon salt
½ teaspoon black pepper
CONTINUED ON NEXT PAGE⮕

PREPARATION

In a food processor or blender, combine tomatoes, onion, and garlic; puree until smooth. Heat 3 tablespoons oil in a heavy 3-quart pot over a medium flame. Sauté oregano and bay leaf for 30 seconds. Add pureed tomato and cook thoroughly, stirring constantly for 2 minutes. Add 8 cups hot water, fish, potatoes, carrots, squash, string beans, olives, jalapeño, salt, and pepper. Bring to a boil, cover, and simmer for 20 minutes or until the potatoes are done. SERVES 6

Tacos de Crema

Cream Tacos

This recipe is actually called an *entomatada*, which roughly translates as a *tomatillo* enchilada, one of many versions you might expect to find in the marketplaces or plazas in and around Guadalajara. My grandmother Delfina's version is by far the best I've ever tasted.

1 quart water
1-½ pounds whole, unhusked *tomatillos*
3 garlic cloves
½ teaspoon salt
1–2 serrano chiles (optional)
1 pound *longaniza* (see note)
¼ cup olive oil
1 dozen corn tortillas
1 white onion, minced fine
¼ cup finely chopped *cilantro*
1 cup lightly whipped *jocoque* or sour cream
4 fresh poblano or Anaheim chiles, roasted, sweated, peeled, seeded, and deveined, cut into strips
Cilantro sprigs, washed and drained

PREPARATION

Blanch the *tomatillos* in 1 quart boiling water for 3 minutes. Drain and save ½ cup of cooking water. Set aside, cool, and remove husks. Place the *tomatillos* in a blender with garlic, salt, and serrano chiles, if desired. Add 3 to 4 tablespoons cooking liquid and blend at high speed for 10 seconds.

Fry the *longaniza* in 1 teaspoon olive oil until completely cooked. Drain, and set aside.

Simmer sauce for 5 minutes in a pan wide enough to dip tortillas.

Heat the remaining oil in a large skillet over a high flame. Dip one tortilla at a time in the hot oil for a few seconds to coat and heat; then dip the tortilla in *tomatillo* sauce. Place on plate and fill with 1 tablespoon *longaniza*, 1 teaspoon minced onion, and ½ teaspoon minced *cilantro*. Roll the tortilla into the shape of an enchilada. Repeat with remaining tortillas. Top with sauce. Spoon sour cream over tacos. Top each enchilada with 3 to 4 strips of green chili and a *cilantro* sprig. Serve immediately.

    Note: *Longaniza*, a sausage similar to *chorizo* made from pork tenderloin, is available at Mexican markets. *Chorizo* may be used as a substitute. Remove the *chorizo* from the plastic casing and sauté in a hot skillet for 5 minutes. Drain *chorizo* on a paper towel.

SERVES 4 TO 6

Guacamole con Semillas de Granada

Delfina's Guacamole with Pomegranate Seeds

The contrast between deep garnet seeds in guacamole green is uniquely festive; the bursts of sour-sweetness mingling with cool avocado and cucumber is unforgettable. Delfina's deceptively simple guacamole perfectly complements my mother's fiery abalone ceviche. Scoop up both with homemade *totopos* or your best store-bought corn chip. We recommend Haas or Fuerte avocados. Avoid using pale-fleshed avocados with low oil content; they lack the taste to stand up to the pomegranate.

2 large ripe Haas or Fuerte avocados, peeled and seeded
2 garlic cloves, pressed in garlic press
1 teaspoon fresh lime juice
¼ cup peeled and finely chopped cucumber
¼ cup cold water
⅓ cup pomegranate seeds
¼ teaspoon salt or to taste

PREPARATION

In a large bowl and using a wooden spoon, mash avocados, garlic, lime juice, and salt until smooth. Fold in cucumbers and slowly add the water. Next fold in pomegranate seeds; be careful not to crush them. Reserve about 1 tablespoon of seeds. To serve, place in a shallow dish. Garnish with pomegranate seeds, making a cross design. Cover and chill before serving.

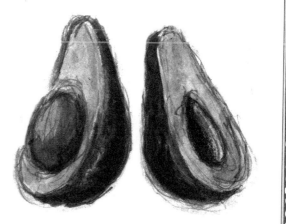

Lengua Rellena Estilo Mérida

Mérida-Style Beef Tongue

My mother learned this recipe from one of her customers at El Adobe, a corpulent Yucatecan woman from Mérida who cooked for a doctor. It was the summer of 1946, a day she remembers for the noisy throng that marched toward the store with Manolete, the legendary Spanish toreador, on their shoulders.

"I was waving at him, the people were totally batty, happy, yelling, 'Manolete! Manolete!, It was very pretty." Just then, her favorite customer walked into the store. My mother, who'd just borne her first child at age twenty without having her parents nearby, enjoyed her motherly advice, her confident dignity, and her recipe for stuffing a tongue, Mérida-style.

When Mary asked my mother to write down this fifty-year-old recipe, she answered, "Come over this evening and I'll show you how to make it." When we arrived, my mother had spread out all the ingredients on her large kitchen table. With instant recall, she explained this recipe step by step. Don't be intimidated by the number of ingredients, she said. Once the tongue is butterflied and vegetables are prepped, the filling process is as easy as making meat loaf, but with a far better result.

PREPPING THE TONGUE

3 pounds raw beef tongue, peeled and butterflied

After peeling the tongue and removing the gristle, make a 1-inch deep slit along the length of the tongue horizontally. Using a very sharp knife, open the tongue up gently on one side and then the other side as if unrolling a roll of paper. Spread it flat, so that it resembles a butterfly with open wings.

FILLING

1 cup ground pork
1 cup ground sirloin
1 egg
1 cup finely chopped yellow onion
1 5-inch cinnamon stick, ground
1-½ teaspoons minced garlic
5 whole cloves, ground
¼ cup diced carrots
½ cup chopped green olives
6 whole black peppercorns, ground
½ cup chopped ham
½ cup chopped and seeded apples
½ cup chopped Italian parsley
¾ cup chopped green onions
¼ cup blanched and peeled chopped almonds
½ cup chopped red pepper
¼ cup raisins
1 tablespoon salt
2 hard-cooked eggs, peeled and whole

PREPARATION

Prepare to stuff the tongue by rubbing it with ½ teaspoon of salt. Mix the filling ingredients and remaining salt in a large bowl, but hold back the hard-cooked eggs. Spread the filling evenly over the tongue to about ½ inch from the edge. Place the two eggs in the center, perpendicular to the wide base end. Tightly roll the tongue up starting at the wider base end toward the tip. Firmly wind a thin string around the entire tongue, securely tying a knot at one end. Set aside.

POT LIQUID

4 cups water
1 yellow onion, quartered
3 ounces Mexican *pilloncillo*
  (break into small pieces) or brown sugar
1 5-inch cinnamon stick
3 bay leaves
5 whole black peppercorns
5 whole cloves
2 garlic cloves
1 tablespoon dry oregano
1 teaspoon salt
2 whole dry *chiles pasillas*
1 cup dry sherry or dry white wine

PREPARATION

Place all ingredients (except the sherry) in a large pot over a high flame and bring to a boil. Add the stuffed beef tongue. Lower the flame to simmer and cover tightly. Cook for 1-½ hours. Add 1 cup dry sherry, cover, and continue to cook for 30 minutes.

Carefully remove the stuffed tongue and place on a large cutting board. Use scissors to cut the strings. Allow the tongue to set for 10 minutes before cutting into ½-inch slices with a very sharp knife. Arrange on a large platter and garnish with parsley. Serve hot or cold.

SERVES 6

in the suburbs:

a woman's education

IF HARD WORK, RESOURCEFULNESS, AND A ferocious independence would come to characterize my father and mother's sojourn in Tijuana, then it came naturally. Both were raised in families with strong work ethics and an ingrained love of business.

In my father's case, these values could be traced back at least three generations to Gregorio, the innkeeper; his wife, Trinidad; his daughter, Catalina; and to my father's own father and mother, Pablo and Delfina. And although the act of crossing the border transformed most Mexicans into workers, families like Delfina's did not forget their social origins. In moving north to California, they would continue to pursue a life of industry, one marked by periods of entrepreneurship, and struggles to pass along their faith in the written word.

Delfina's granddaughter, Graciela, born June 28, 1931, both witnessed and learned from her grandmother's struggles. Delfina not only taught her to read and write, she also revealed to Graciela her place in a genealogy of memory. But until I'd visited her, no one had ever asked Graciela to put her experiences into words. Her recollections begin in 1939, when Delfina persuaded her son-in-law, Julio, to take over a tiny grocery store in Downey, California.

My grandmother "was the one who would say 'Let's get into business, let's buy this property,'" Graciela said. "My dad was very conservative when it came to money matters." About a year later, Delfina, with her daughter Estela's help, persuaded Julio to open another store in Canta Ranas, then a community of swayback houses built of creosote-stained railroad ties for the families of orange pickers. They rented a house across the street from their store.

From such modest beginnings a family extended branches that continued forking. The couple would raise six children, bury one of them, send some to college, buy property, build on it, remodel, and keep their doors open for relatives who'd had enough of Guadalajara. Over the years, we knew that their kitchen or sitting room was there for us, a clearinghouse of relations where we could recover a sense of continuity by visiting with family ghosts.

More than just encouraging family members to go into business for themselves, Delfina, despite her advancing age, would frequently roll up her sleeves and work herself. At other times, she shouldered the housekeeping and parenting duties, which gave her daughter and grand-daughters the freedom to work outside the home, and so improve upon their roles as daughters, wives, and mothers.

"She would encourage my mother to work. They took turns being the caretakers. I remember Mother not working at times, and then my grandmother working. And you know, we never called her Grandmother. We called her Mama Delfina. My mother was Mama Estela. So it was always the two mothers," remembers Graciela.

Freeing Estela to sew in a garment factory increased the family's income, but only because Delfina promoted herself as unofficial house-mother, taking charge of domestic matters, an authority she asserted whenever she made plans for the next meal.

"I can remember being at the table and already talking about the preparations for the next meal," began Graciela's younger sister. "'We've got to soak this overnight.' That went on all the time. My mother didn't particularly like to cook, so she'd say, 'You've just finished eating and already you're talking about the next meal.'"

In some ways, the arrangement provided Delfina the kind of household she had been raised to rule. Although Delfina could be domineering, and was at times resented for this, Graciela says that she now appreciates the special atmosphere her grandmother nurtured: "In our family we never experienced any of this machismo that a lot of people in the U.S. correlate with Mexico. In our family the maternal influence was stronger, starting with my grandmother."

Distance from Mexico also gave Mexican women a greater freedom to govern their own thoughts and personal affairs.

"My mother and grandmother were never religious fanatics," Graciela confesses. "I remember my mother saying, 'Oh, this not eating meat on Friday, how can God say this? You know what, the Pope probably has a fish concession.' My mother and my grandmother used to say, 'Those are church rules and not God's rules,' even with contraception. My mother practiced contraception because she didn't feel it was one of God's rules."

Their renegotiation of religion also took a philosophical turn. Mama Delfina would render advice by prefacing it with, "If there is a hell..."

"If there is a hell, then bad people will be punished. If there isn't, then this is all we have and bad people should be punished here on earth."

It amazed her granddaughters that Delfina entertained doubts on such basic articles of faith. But years later, they realized that their grandmother had, by expressing doubt, given them permission to entertain their own.

Delfina also taught Graciela something about

cooking, but the lessons of the kitchen aren't the ones that linger in her memory. No, she remembers her grandmother teaching her to read and write in Spanish, formal language skills that made learning English easy, she said. And she remembers the stories she told of another time, and other women.

GRACIELA NOW REALIZES THAT SHE'D ENTERED into a relationship with her grandmother that nurtured her intellectual growth and preserved her Mexican heritage.

"My mother and my grandmother, especially my grandmother, were always saying, 'Don't let anybody call you anything but Graciela; don't let them call you Grace.'"

The "them" in this case were her Anglo classmates who held their own ideas of what a Mexican could and could not be; a smart teacher's pet didn't fit their expectations. So they asked her if she would consider trading her identity for one more in line with her talents. "I always used to get, 'Yeah, but you're different. You're not Mexican, or you don't look Mexican.'" Yet she never considered it an option. She knew her parents and grandmother would have been outraged had she even considered the offer.

Her older aunts and uncles mocked those who tried to pass for Spanish, even though some of them could have; their nationalism would not let them indulge such fantasies. Delfina, for her part, reminded Graciela of the outrages the Spanish had committed against the Indians of Mexico, and that, by being her granddaughter, she shared her Indian blood. Delfina, in telling this, wasn't strain-ing for melodrama. Compared to other members of our family, Delfina was dark, unmistakably *mestiza*. And because Delfina could read and had been raised by teachers, books and schools neither mystified nor frightened her. Nor did she hesitate to correct the lies she discovered in Graciela's textbooks.

"One time I brought home a social studies book, and one of the stories said that they threw in dirty socks into the *pulque* so that it would start to ferment," Graciela said. "I remember that very clearly because she was so angry.

"'How could they write this?' she'd say. 'Don't you believe it! You have to be very discriminating about what you read.'"

For a child who wanted to be reassured about her English-speaking world, Delfina's lessons must have seemed bitter ones. By contradicting her teachers, and challenging the truth in her books, Delfina put her teacher's lessons in a critical light. She also encouraged her to place her two languages and literatures, English and Spanish, on an equal footing.

Nor did Delfina buy the arguments of cultural assimilation, which required that Mexicans jettison their Spanish. Culturally, at least, she already believed herself to be as mainstream as you could want. And she just took the universality of her language for granted. Though she didn't pretend to be a great intellect, she knew the Spanish language had produced a literature that belonged to the world. The question was, would her descendants still speak and write Spanish — a goal she believed completely consistent with a well-rounded education. A halfway decent school system should at least be able to teach students to be fully literate in two languages. After all, Catalina spoke French and some English. To expect less, especially of her grandchildren, would be to make them intellectual invalids in the name of creating loyal citizens.

She preferred to hold to the faith that literacy, no matter the languages learned, was never an impediment. Her certainty came from experience. To embark upon the self-improving project of eduation was an article of faith for Mexico's nineteenth-century middle class. That was Catalina's lesson to Delfina. She had invented herself through education, not from unearned privileges or inherited money. Sadly, however, the Anglo-run schools weren't ready to understand that Delfina shared their values, just in another language. So it was her job to counsel patience and remind her grandchildren of her pact with language. She did this by needling my father with questions. Had he kept up with Spanish lessons for my sisters and me? We were expected to repay the investment by reciting maudlin and modernist verses to her as she sat in a folding chair in a park on Mother's Day, gratified at the procession of reluctant gift-givers.

Living as she did, under Delfina's watchful presence, Graciela felt compelled, even pressured, to attend college at a time when few other Latinas could or dared. "I always felt like I had to go to college, that I had to do well, because my grandmother expected it," she says.

Eventually, Graciela attended California State University, Los Angeles, in 1952, where she earned her B.A. Then Graciela had to make a choice—marry her present husband, Luis, or go on for a teaching credential. Although Mama Delfina and Mama Estela recommended against it, Graciela chose marriage, which disappointed her mother. Delfina, thinking of her own solitude, reminded Estela that her daughter's personal happiness should not be ignored. So Graciela gave birth to her first child, then another, and another. She then began to question whether she'd made the right choices. At one point, she saw herself falling into deep depression when she felt the possibility of resuming her career slipping from her grasp.

"I began to feel very disappointed," she said. "I felt I needed to get back to work, that I needed more of a mental challenge." That's when Delfina intervened. She offered to quit her job as a seamstress to care for the children if Graciela went back to school. Graciela agreed. Since she still had a family to raise and a husband who needed her, her education and career zigzagged between the births of six children, college classes, and her first teaching jobs.

Finally, with the support of her husband and children, and about twenty years as the head of two Head-Start programs, Graciela earned her credential in 1991, which allowed her to teach kindergarten until her retirement three years later. To an outsider, Graciela's experience would appear to confirm the trajectory of the stereotypical immigrant's progress, which is traced in an ascending line that begins in foreign humble origins and ends in middle-class smugness. But a spiral would be more accurate, since hers was not a heroic struggle against insurmountable odds, but a lifetime's slow circling ascent. By becoming a teacher, Graciela reclaimed Catalina's achievements for herself, but not without Delfina at her side.

"She would always tell us," Graciela says, "to be proud of the fact that you're a descendant of the Vargas family. She would talk a lot about Catalina, that she was very intelligent, that the whole family was proud of her because she'd been the principal of an elementary school and because she was a writer."

Graciela paused, her eyes on the verge of welling up, as if relieved at finally having said it all, and broken a spell. Now she needed to show me something. I looked out to the pool outside her patio, almost obliterated by the atomizing light of late morning. She walked back with an oval portrait—Catalina as a girl of ten, painted around 1872. She placed it on the table. Picking it up, I noticed its lightness, and the tiny dark specks of desicated worm excrement spill like sand from its scrolled frame.

The frame has been repaired so many times that the portrait's protective sheet of oval glass no longer fits. I held it over Catalina's face to see how she originally appeared. Its hand-poured imperfections—countless tiny elongated bubbles frozen in a faintly blue pane—gave me the eerie feeling of a face rising up from the depths.

Graciela, at age twenty-five, had asked her mother for the portrait soon after the birth of her third child. The birth came at a moment when she feared sinking into domestic oblivion. And the portrait, she believed, would help her to regain momentum and a sense of focus. Catalina's plump cheeks, her broad square forehead, and upward-gazing eyes told Graciela she had to have the portrait. My aunt needed Catalina's example. Graciela said her youthful guardian reminded her of her own worth and promise, of the chain of knowledge linking her to a line of strong-willed women. Sitting across from her, her eyes told me she'd honored her promise. Graciela's persistence had encouraged her four daughters to follow her example, and become schoolteachers like Catalina.

PORTRAIT OF CATALINA
AT TEN YEARS OLD, CIRCA 1872,
PAINTED IN TEMPERA.

children of mayaguel

But the true drinkers are the aged men,
the aged women and the adventurers, the daring,
those who never give into fear,
those who throw their hearts and heads into the game.

FRAY BERNARDINO DE SAHAGUN
sixteenth-century Spanish chronicler of New Spain

NOT ALL THE RECIPES DELFINA BROUGHT with her from Mexico were written in cookbooks. She scribbled some on loose sheets of paper she dated May 23, 1908, about a year before she married.

One such recipe stands out. It was titled *Lomo en Frío con Pulque* (Cold Roast Beef in a *Pulque* Sauce). *Pulque*, the fermented juice of the agave cactus, commonly known as a century plant, comes to our time right out of Jalisco's pre-Hispanic past. I found it intriguing, but without a supply of *pulque* I assumed the recipe would have to go untested. That's about as far as my curiosity went, at least until my uncle Teófilo called me up on the telephone one May morning in 1982 to show me how the past hides in the present, until summoned forth in recollection.

TEÓFILO, MY UNCLE JULIO'S YOUNGER BROTHER, had promised a few months before that he'd show me how to make *pulque* the next time he cracked one of the *magueyes* growing like a huge forbidding pineapple bush in his backyard in La Mirada, a placid Southern California suburb a few miles north of Orange County. For years, I heard my relatives talk about *pulque* with either disgust or yearning, but I didn't really expect Teófilo to show me what all the fuss was about. Still, I was curious enough to find out. And anyway, I thought it might make an interesting feature for the *Los Angeles Times*, where I worked in one of the paper's suburban sections.

I got to his house at about 9 A.M., the time he planned to "crack" the *maguey*. We walked into his patio, where Teófilo showed me his tools, which lay somewhere under the mountains of junk he sold at swap meets. He slowly slid boxes of dusty jars as he struggled to rearrange the antlered aluminum of broken lawn furniture. His eyes, now fading to gray, carefully followed his hands in the triangular shadows created by the *chayote* vine. Rising from the patio's dirt floor, its heavy net of

lime leaves camouflaged his garage, and clung to his kitchen window. Finally, he straightened himself. In his hands he held a small half moon saw and large, spoonlike blade for reaching and piercing the *maguey*'s white membranous skull.

He then approached the near-tree-size *maguey*. It filled a whole corner of his backyard like some

previous page: MY LATE UNCLE TEÓFILO SAWING OFF THE MAGUEY'S JIOTE, SUMMER, 1987, THE BACKYARD OF HIS LA MIRADA HOME.

above: TEÓFILO CARVING THE MAGUEY IN PREPARATION FOR EXTRACTING AGUAMIEL.

beast bristling with black thorns. He carefully lodged boards between its blue-gray leaves, making a ladder to climb between the small black shark's teeth that gird each leaf, then reached down to the *mezontle*, the boulder-shaped mass of stored juices, and cut the first leaf.

"Cut only a few," he said, "to save *aguamiel*," the honey-sweet sap the *maguey* "cries" after being wounded. "This is *jiote*," he added, a spike rising from the *mezontle*'s core. This shaft of unfurled leaves grows three houses high before it blossoms bitter, sulfurous flowers that announce the *maguey's* death. He sawed it off at the base, carved a small pocket to fibrous whiteness, a shade which the Aztecs compared to the full moon. Next he filled the cavity with the shavings, and covered it with a smooth round stone to keep insects from fouling the brew. He'd return the next morning to start the bleeding, first ladling out the *aguamiel* that had collected overnight, then carefully scraping away the thin membrane the plant had woven to heal itself. He'd repeat the routine twice a day, making sure the wound stayed fresh, initially extracting *aguamiel* by the pint, and then, after several weeks, by the half gallon.

Teófilo reminded me just how different two brothers can be. At age eight, my uncle Julio was sent to San Pedro Tlaquepaque to begin his schooling with Catalina. Julio so thoroughly adopted city ways that it would be impossible for me to imagine him, years later, at a beach picnic in anything but a tailored suit, tie, and gray fedora. Teófilo stayed behind on the family hacienda in Jalisco, learning the region's indigenous plant lore, waiting several years before following his brothers to Los Angeles. He died in 1986 at age eighty-seven. Everything about his appearance marked him as a descendant of Jalisco's Spanish settlers, but everything he taught me about *magueyes* that morning came from its indigenous inhabitants.

He told me that no part of the *maguey*—its leaves, juices, flowers, roots, and thorns—is wasted. *Pulque*, a syrupy wine, is fermented from the *maguey*'s cinnamon-colored juices. The ancient Mexicans also concentrated the unfermented mead into candy; honey was made from its pollen-rich flowers; its large, tuberlike roots were roasted and chewed, and its long thorns became sewing needles. Today, whole *maguey* leaves are still placed in underground barbeque pits. The hot embers make these leaves release their sweet cactus flavor into linen bags holding joints of goat, pork, or beef flavored with chiles and spices. And a tough, parchmentlike material removed from inside the leaf is used for wrapping and steaming pieces of lamb or kid in a delicacy called *mixiotes*.

Anthropologists credit the *maguey* as the unsung lifesaver of Mesoamerican agriculture. *Aguamiel* and *pulque* provided a reliable alternative to water for the peasants during the dry season when shortages of drinking water would have otherwise made work in the fields impossible. Just as importantly, *aguamiel* and *pulque* are foods.

A bit more than six ounces of *pulque*, or 200 grams, provides 13 percent of the U.S.-recommended daily allowance for thiamine, 4 percent of riboflavin, and 5 percent of niacin. The same serving is also high in calcium, exceeding the recommended daily allowance of 1 milligram, and contains 20 percent of the recommended allow-ance for vitamin C and 4 percent of the allowance for iron. Compared to 200 grams of orange juice, *pulque* is slightly higher in B vitamins and iron, moderately higher in phosphorus and potassium, but lower in vitamin C.

Due to natural organisms living within the *maguey*, fermentation is already under way when the juice is extracted, turning *aguamiel* into *pulque* within twenty-four hours. *Pulque* can reach an alcohol content ranging between 8 percent and 10 percent within eighteen days of aging, which explains why *pulque* drinking in pre-Columbian times was strictly regulated. Most people drank *aguamiel* the way we drink milk today. *Pulque* was reserved for the Aztec priests and warriors as a ceremonial intoxicant. The elderly also were permitted to indulge, as long as they did so in the privacy of their homes. But apparently, *pulque* drinking occasionally led to excess, usually when the elderly took their drunkenness into the streets and marketplaces. So the Aztecs devised a ruthlessly efficient way of handling their elderly inebriates—they simply carved out the aged offender's heart on the sacrificial stone.

Still, the ancient Mexicans venerated the *maguey* for its life-sustaining and intoxicating virtues. *Pulque*, the Aztecs believed, was the milk of Mayaguel, the Goddess of One Hundred Breasts who ruled the heaven of drowned children and mothers who died in childbirth. In the Aztec codices, or picture books, she is depicted as a large *maguey* with several breasts from which drowned children suckle in the shade of her leaves. Teófilo, however, didn't have to die to taste the tree of the afterlife.

"I was eleven when I knew *pulque*," Teófilo said the day he taught me to tap his *maguey*. "Hell! Once my uncle Nacho told me, 'You are too poor. I'll give you some tools because the *magueyes* are going bad, shooting up their spikes. Crack *magueyes* and sell *pulque*.' Nacho gave me the faculties to do this.

"Over in the big pasture, there must have been three hundred of them" that had grown into a thorny barrier. "They were mean ones, some tall ones. At least eight liters of *aguamiel* they gave each day. Between my brothers and I and two others, we cracked sixty in one blow. Then seventy more. The biggest ones, the prettiest ones. I would find them sloppy with *aguamiel*. And I, sucking *magueyes*, drinking four liters a day," he recounted. "It tasted like *panocha* [raw sugar] with cinnamon, delicious."

He continued extracting *aguamiel* and brewing *pulque*. He boasted of drinking more than a quart of *pulque* each day that summer. He would dilute it with some previously boiled water and loads of crushed ice, and then flavor it with finely diced oranges, onions, and ground toasted *chile piquín*, or with finely diced pineapple or the plump yellow, pink-fleshed *guayabas* from his yard. He'd tell me it made his blood strong. But I think he loved *pulque* because of all the attention it brought him.

Each afternoon during that summer, young and mature men, mostly old work mates from Jalisco thirsty for a taste of home, drove up to Teófilo's house for a drink. Or else it was their wives or sisters who came with empty plastic milk containers. They wanted to get away from kids or a sweltering kitchen and sip something cool under the tree in Teófilo's front yard. They'd pay him a nominal fee for his trouble. The transaction, of course, was illegal, but it allowed them to indulge in a few icy glassfuls of *pulque*, which they would sip while sitting on old lawn furniture, each remembering the shade of other trees, of other childhoods. Yet these immigrants, the children of Mayaguel, did not just thirst for memories, but also a way to honor and preserve them.

But they themselves were too busy working, and their lives too unsettled, to wait a decade for their own *magueyes* to mature. Only someone from another century, with time on his hands, like Teófilo, could dedicate himself to their memories. So they drank as long as the *pulque* lasted, relishing the flavors of conversation and of childhood.

Lomo en Frío con Pulque

Cold Roast Beef in a Pulque Sauce

Canned pasturized *pulque* can be purchased in border towns like Tijuana or Juarez. If that's too far to drive, then use a Pilsen-type beer instead.

3-½ pounds top round roast or any quality lean
    beef roast
2 cups *pulque,* or a Pilsen-type beer
3 1-inch cinnamon sticks
3 bay leaves
1 teaspoon whole black peppercorns
½ cup chopped white onion
1 cup finely diced tomatoes
6 whole cloves
3 teaspoons salt
2 teaspoons olive oil
½ white onion, sliced into ⅛-inch rings
1 head butter or romaine lettuce, washed
    and drained
2 tablespoons chopped Spanish capers
¼ cup whole Spanish green olives
7 yellow pickled chiles

PREPARATION

On the day before cooking, place the roast in a deep roasting pan. In a medium bowl, mix *pulque*, cinnamon, bay leaves, peppercorns, onions, tomatoes, cloves, and salt. Rub the spices and *pulque* into the meat. Cover and marinate overnight in the refrigerator. Preheat oven to 350 degrees. Cook roast for 1-½ hours. The meat should be slightly pink. Separate the roast from the pan juices and allow it to cool. Heat the olive oil in a large skillet over a medium flame. Sauté the onion rings, then add ¾ cups of strained meat juices and sauté for 2 minutes.

    Place the roast on a large cutting board and cut into thin ⅛-inch slices and place on a platter lined with the lettuce leaves. Pour the warm sautéed onion sauce over the meat. Decorate with capers, olives, and chiles.

SERVES 5 TO 6

the persistence of purslane

I'D DROPPED IN WITH ESTELA TO ASK A FEW few more questions. Estela answered what she could before reminding me it was time for lunch.

So I sat at her dining-room table, within hearing distance of her tiny kitchen. Like the house, it was new; new chrome faucet fixtures and glossy counter tiles. But the new kitchen was smaller than the old one in their first house next door where her mother, Delfina, used to cook. New also was the view from her dining-room window. Beyond the blinds stood roses, daisies, and ferns almost obliterated by light, and a plaster birdbath framed by a carpet of Saint Augustine lawn. The houses on her street had been remodeled or rebuilt, giving it the orderly aspect of a place where people cared about appearances. No trace of dusty alleys prowled by angry dogs or the store where I had tasted Catalina's squab recipe as a child.

Meanwhile, Estela reminisced as she chopped onion, trimmed pork ribs, and mashed cloves of garlic. She then placed these ingredients in a medium pot half filled with cold water with a small bay leaf, and a pinch of cumin seeds. She put a lid on the pot, brought it to a simmer, then came back to her chair in the dining room. Had I followed her into the kitchen, I would have noticed the maroon bowl of chile paste. Prior to my arrival she had toasted, seeded, soaked, and ground some *guajillo* and California chiles—a combination with which you would season a pot of *posole*.

In the meantime, she answered a telephone call, got up to check her pot, chatted, and coaxed her Yellowhead Amazon parrot to sing a few bars of "*Se fue*" ("He's Left"). An enjoyable visit, though I wasn't getting much done. Then something that sounded vaguely familiar to me caught Estela's attention. Outside, a man's voice approaching from a distance barked some gravelly words into his bullhorn. She grabbed her purse and walked out the front door as fast as her legs allowed. *"Ahorita vuelvo* (I'll be right back)." I looked through the blinds. She ambled stiffly out to midstreet to join a group of women who'd gathered around the rear gate of a large new truck. It was the *verdurero*, the vegetable peddler, placing something inside a scale that hung from the ceiling of his large white trailer.

A common sight in Mexican neighborhoods. When I was a kid, the *verdureros* cruised our street just before dinner, breaking up our baseball game, and giving our mothers a chance to beckon with a dollar bill raised in one hand, shouting, "Ask him if he has radishes," or "Look at the *cilantro,"* which was a polite way of asking us to check if it was wilted. The *verdureros* still cruised streets like Estela's, selling big, fragrant, Nayarit mangoes, some green splashed with orange, others orange splashed with red; ripe blackening plantains; small pungent Mexican limes; or dusky rough-skinned avocados that yield to the touch. Then I realized the tropics had also invaded the uptown Whittier neighborhood where I then lived.

Only a few days ago, I'd bought a *paleta de tamarindo,* or popsicle of deliciously sour and sweet tamarind pulp, from a *paletero* who'd pushed his two-wheeled cart from who knows where to the sidewalk in front of my house. Hours in the sun pushing his cart, had darkened the man, made him lean. He reminded me of other *paleteros*, ones we stopped as kids in front of Delfina's house in Rosarito Beach, then a sleepy resort south of Tijuana. We had to squint hard through freezing vapors to pick out *paletas* made of guava, banana,

hybiscus, strawberry, mango, or coconut. This was one of several situations where my sister Christina and I would have to speak Spanish during our vacations — part of the involuntary language immersions orchestrated by Delfina and our parents. I remember the *paletas de tamarindo,* and the mysteries of finding the button-size mahogany-colored seeds locked inside a coffee-colored popsicle. Now a *palatero* sold the same popsicles on my street. I stood on the sidewalk

PHOTO OF ESTELA AND JULIO ON THEIR WEDDING DAY, CIRCA 1930.

in front of my house with my daughters, each of us savoring the tamarind's sweet-sour flavor while a flock of Mexican parakeets screeched overhead, their emerald-ribboned tail feathers trailing into my neighbor's tree. These escapees from the cages of bird smugglers reminded me of the *palatero.* Both had found their niche on my tree-shaded street.

Estela walked into the dining room, gently

twisting a bundle of *verdolagas*, or purslane, as it is also known, in the air. Her gesture expressed admiration at the huge teardrop leaves, a shiny deep olive color bursting from pale green purslane stalks tinged with crimson. Optimum growing conditions in the fields made the weed at least three times larger than its normal size, though they still tasted of watercress and Swiss chard. The most common species, *Portulaca oleracea*, came across the Atlantic from Europe in the 1670s, spreading its networks of juicy branches throughout North America, until arriving in Estela's pot, where it simmered beautifully with New World chiles.

Part herb, part vegetable, and part weed, the *verdolaga* is a classic opportunist. It thrives in freshy tilled, irrigated soils, choking up furrows ploughed for other crops. Its succulent leaves and stems not only store water like drought-resistant cacti, it also produces thousands of minute seeds that germinate as soon as they mature. The weed, which has crossed borders and oceans, has spread so fast it's become the nemesis of North American farmers and gardeners.

But as strange as it may seem, a few farmers grow it for Mexicans and trendy restaurants that use it to dress up salads and flavor stews the way cooks in France, the Mediterranean, and the tropics have done for ages. Although sold by supermarkets and farmers' markets throughout Southern California, it's hard to say exactly how much is grown—purposely, that is. Obviously, not enough to concern the California Department of Agriculture, or even compete with the harvest and multimillion-dollar sales of *tomatillo* or fresh chile, which, in California alone, totaled $30.8 million in 1992.

Yet its "discovery" by nutritionists and trend-setting chefs promise to change all this. Recent studies show purslane to be the highest vegetable source of the heart-saving Omega-3 fatty acids found in salmon; it also packs three times the Vitamin E found in spinach. And its tangy watercress flavor has prompted some chefs to proclaim it the radicchio of the '90s.

But making a culinary fashion statement was the furthest from Estela's mind when she watched the *verdolagas* sink into the steaming broth before she added another handful. That was it, five minutes' cooking at most. Estela served me a bowlful accompanied by a basket of steaming corn tortillas. I didn't know what to admire more. Estela's timing, the plate she placed before me, or the patience and generosity she'd always shown me. The bold warming flavors of sweet, full-bodied piquancy and the lemony *verdolaga* tang and agreeable bitterness reminded me of watercress in a Cantonese broth sweetened with pork and ginger. Then I realized that Estela, who stayed out of the kitchen while her mother was alive, had imprinted me with her own culinary memory.

Verdolagas con Costillitas de Puerco

Purslane and Pork Ribs Soup

Estela learned this recipe from her mother, Delfina. It's one of many variations of Jalisco's *posole*-like soups seasoned with ground chile. If purslane is not available, substitute with an equal quantity of watercress.

1 teaspoon olive oil
4 California chile pods, washed, seeded, and deveined
2 *guajillo* pods washed, seeded, and deveined
2 cups hot water (reserve 1 cup soaking solution)
1 teaspoon white wine vinegar
1-½ pounds country-style pork spareribs, trimmed, cut into big chunks
2 medium garlic cloves, crushed
1 bay leaf
¼ teaspoon cumin seed
1 medium onion, halved
5-½ cups water
3 teaspoons salt
8–10 ounces purslane, rinsed and drained, cut   into 5-inch lengths

PREPARATION

Heat olive oil in a medium skillet over a medium flame. Sauté chile pods for 30 seconds. Soak the chiles in hot water and vinegar for 1 hour. Reserve 1 cup soaking solution, and set aside. Place hydrated chile skins in a blender with about 1 cup soaking solution, and blend until smooth. Makes about 1-½ cups chile paste.

Place pork, garlic, bay leaf, cumin, onion and salt in a medium pot with 5-½ cups water, bring to a boil, then cover, lower heat, and simmer for 45 minutes. (You may wish to cool the cooked meat and broth before skimming off excess fat.) Add 1 cup of the chile paste to the soup stock, reserve the rest in the refrigerator. Cover and simmer about 10 minutes over a medium flame.

Uncover and bring the stock to a gentle boil before adding half the purslane to the soup; wait a minute or so before adding the rest. Cover and simmer another 10 minutes before serving. SERVES 4 TO 5

a cuisine without borders:

a culture with two countries

THE IDEA THAT PURSLANE, OR THE *VER-DOLAGA* (see Chapter Sixteen), might find a place in the supermarket produce section next to the *cilantro* and *jalapeños* strikes me as ironic. Less than a century ago, the first Anglos to arrive in California viewed Mexican cuisine with suspicion; some even considered it poisonous. If this sounds outlandish, then consider the story published in the May 13, 1899 edition of the *Los Angeles Record*, then the city's most liberal newspaper.

Miss Maude Hufford, one of the handsomest girls in Los Angeles, has been lying at the point of death since early last Sunday morning. Her condition is due to ptomaine poisoning, produced by a tamale that was composed of putrified meat.

The twenty-one-year-old shopgirl had sent out for some tamales at lunchtime. But soon after eating, Miss Hufford "suffered terrible agony, even though unconscious. Every joint in her body became stiffened, and it was necessary constantly to massage her with hot alcohol and move each joint every two hours. Yesterday morning she emerged from the comatose condition and was able to speak a few words."

There's no proof that a "putrified" tamale was responsible for Hufford's poisoning, but this fact did not stop the *Record*'s reporter from leveling accusations: "Bad meat is often used in the manufacture of tamales, the offensive taste being disguised by the fiery condiments which are used."

Miss Hufford, whom the reporter described as "a most pronounced blonde" with "beautiful flaxen hair, a pearly complexion and large expressive blue eyes," may have indeed ingested a tainted tamale, but the reporter's effort to convict a cuisine by means of racist analogy is self-evident. This flaxen-haired beauty, the image of Anglo racial purity, was stricken by deceptive spices and "bad meat," the reporter's shorthand for racial defilement.

Not all Californian characterizations of Mexican cuisine since Miss Hufford's time have been so explicitly vicious. But this fact does not change the final result. For much of the early part of this century, several factors converged to effectively demonize or distort the image of Mexican culture and cuisine. They called it "Spanish" when they wished to appropriate what they liked, and "Mexican" when they needed to disparage it.

If one searches the publishing history of Mexican food in California, it is not too difficult to find examples of such culinary revisionism. Encarnación Piñedo's *El Cocinero Español* has the rare distinction of not only being California's first Spanish-language cookbook, but one of its most paradoxical editions. For its time and many years afterward, Piñedo's book was the most sophisticated volume on Mexican cuisine, in spite of its title. Dan Strehl, a senior librarian at the Los Angeles City Library and translator of sixty of Piñedo's recipes, has noted that her recipes are heirs to Mexico's nineteenth-century cuisine with its "distinctive Spanish, Indian, and French influences." Piñedo's *Mole de carnero*, or lamb mole, for example, is a virtual word-for-word copy of Catalina's *Mole caraqueño de carnero*, itself a copy of a recipe published in a Mexican cookbook in 1853. The beginnings of California cuisine can also be detected in her liberal use of fruits and vegetables, fresh edible flowers and herbs, her aggressive spicing, and grilling over native wood fires.

Despite the debt her recipes owe to Mexican cuisine, Piñedo had the habit of giving them names that suggested Iberian origins. For example, her *Guajolote en mole gallego* (Turkey in a

Galician Mole) is a simplified version of the Mexican original. Why Hispanicize the names of Mexican recipes, or disguise the fact that her "Spanish" cooking was inextricably rooted in Mexican cuisine? Much of the answer, I believe, lies on the Berreyesa branch of Piñedo's family tree.

From 1846 to 1856, Yankee miners and vigilantes had lynched or shot a total of eight of her closest male relatives, all Berreyesas, and none for good reasons. Crooked land lawyers and squatters also reduced one of the most land-rich California families—an estimated 160,000 acres—to poverty. Landless, broke, and mired in litigation, the seventy-member Berreyesa clan had no choice but to beg the San José town government for a small plot to build new homes. Not surprisingly, Piñedo's mother, María Del Carmen Berreyesa, forbid her daughters to talk to, let alone marry, the gringos who'd murdered her grandfather and uncles. Piñedo would see her sister and six nieces defy her mother's wishes and marry Yankee newcomers. Piñedo, herself, would eventually accept the victor's version of history. "Silver-toned bells come with the light of the Gospel all the way from Old Spain," she wrote in one article, invoking the romantic image of California as a Spanish idyll. Of course, not all of California's culinary literature bought into the Spanish-Mission mythology. Eleven years after the publication of Piñedo's *Cocinero*, in 1909, California's first bilingual cookbook, *Recipes from Old Mexico*, was published. May Middleton, who translated recipes she collected during a trip to Mexico, offers a small but authentic selection.

But according to Strehl, such acknowledgments were rare and late in coming.

In his search of library databases, he found more than 1,900 citations of books on California cookery. Of these, only 44, or about 2 percent, are dedicated in part or in full to Mexican or Spanish cuisine, and only eight were written by identifiable Spanish-surnamed authors. After Piñedo's *El Cocinero Español*, the next full-length Mexican cookbook written by a Spanish-surnamed writer does not appear until 1944. Most Mexican recipes were compiled by Anglo women's church or social groups in sections dedicated to "Spanish" recipes, or else published in trade books, such as *California's Mission Recipes*, which stress the romantic "Old Spanish" days. At the very least, Strehl said, the quality and quantity of the publishing record reveals the lack of importance given to the Mexican contribution to California cuisine. But it says more than that. A publishing history also reveals the resources and ideas with which a community represents its culinary culture. And for much of this history, the Mexican community has lacked the resources to publish interpretations of its culinary memory.

Today, however, the recently published Mexican cookbooks stocked in bookstore shelves would appear to have sideswiped the cuisine's former image. The same goes for the consumption of Mexican food. Both trends suggest that Latino cuisine has finally been accepted into the nation's mainstream culture. Take, for starters, the meteoric rise in salsa sales.

Americans now drop more bottles of salsa and picante sauces in their shopping carts than ketchup. Packaged Facts, Inc. reports that the turning point came in 1991, when combined salsa/picante sales increased by 24 percent and totaled $640 million, compared to ketchup sales of $600 million. Since then, the New York-based research firm has reported that salsa/picante sales have grown at an 8 to 12 percent rate until last year, when they reached $940 million. Combined salsa/picante sales should pick up again this year and continue at a double-digit clip through 1999, when salsa/picante sales are projected to reach $1.56 billion. Salsa sales mirror a wider trend. Packaged Facts has projected retail sales of Mexican food of $2.4 billion in 1994, and $3.45 billion in 1999.

Marketing analysts say several factors converged to promote the popularity of Mexican food, or the salsafication of the American diet. You might think of the 22.4 million Latinos, who can be found from Washington, D.C. to Los Angeles, as the spark that spread the fire of Mexican food beyond its traditional Southwestern hearth place. Consumers from Seattle to Boston have added Pace Thick & Chunky Picante Sauce and McDonald's breakfast burritos to their diets. You can even find taco trucks in Manhattan. Selling salsa and corn tortillas as the low-fat and low-calorie diet foods of the '80s also reduced, if only slightly, Mexican food's greasy image. The glitzy marketing of that hard-to-define entity called Southwest cuisine made Mexican food less foreign, or more American.

Before you knew it, even non-Mexican restaurants such as Pizzeria Uno added chicken fajitas to their menus. Salsa craving and the new menu items, in turn, boosted the demand for other Mexican foods, especially tortillas, which reported sales of more than $1.09 billion in 1991. No doubt the recession in the late '80s pushed consumers to hunt for bargains and comfort, which, in the '90s, means simple, healthful cooking with bolder flavors. Mexican food meets these criteria, says David Weiss, president of Packaged Facts, because of what he calls the "idiot-proof factor."

"Some cuisines, such as French and Japanese, do not suffer inept preparation or food processing very well, and that's why their restaurant popularity has never been equaled by retail sales," wrote Weiss. "But Mexican food is pretty tasty, no matter what you do to it."

I know of no surveys showing that consumers prefer Mexican food because it suffers mediocrity well. But the surveys do show why the eating public prefers Mexican fast food—it's cheap and it's familiar. Bargain-hungry consumers, including Latinos who know better, flock to Taco Bell, which reported 1994 sales of $3.4 billion, up 17 percent from 1993, because it's the last place where they can afford to eat out, even if it's just to munch on a 59-cent taco.

But there are limits. Karen Caplan, president of Frieda's Finest Inc., purveyor of tropical fruits and vegetables that brought us the kiwi, and now zapotes, says the *verdolaga* will never follow the taco's example. Purslane, she says, is simply too perishable for widespread distribution. Other growers say they'll continue to grow it, but only as a boutique vegetable. They say the *verdolaga*, like so many other Mexican foods, stubbornly resists mass marketing.

So now two strains of Mexican food flourish on this side of the border—mass-produced fast Cal- or Tex-Mex food, and epicurean specialties, like *verdolaga* and *chipolte* chiles. And while gourmet interpretations of Mexican cuisine may be on the rise, it's the demands of the former, not the latter, that continue to dominate the market image of Mexican cuisine. The cost of producing perfectly U-shaped taco shells and other such oddities has been quite high. The industrial transformation of Mexican food has thus made it an easy target for consumer groups such as the Center for Science in the Public Interest, which recently issued a report criticizing Mexican restaurant fare of the midpriced and fast-food varieties for being too high in calories, fat, and salt. What were the offending foods?

Not Estela's *verdolaga* recipe, not the numerous vegetable-, grain-, and legume-based recipes low in fats or salt commonly found in the first-generation Mexican immigrants' diet, but the usual combination-plate suspects: A pair of cheese enchiladas, refried beans and rice (totaling 1,349 calories, 68 grams of fat, and 2,878 milligrams of salt), or two *chiles rellenos*, no doubt the kind carpeted with oil-soaked egg white, rice, and refried beans (totaling 1,578 calories, 96 grams of fat, and 3,352 milligrams of salt), both of which exceed the 65-gram recommended daily limit for fat and 2,400-milligram maximum recommended daily limits for salt.

Interpreting the report as an attack, a few Latinos sallied forth to defend their culinary honor. Yet they'd missed the point. These defenders failed to stress the nutritional strengths of

Mexican food, particularly the recent immigrant's diet, which tends to be high in grains, fruits, vegetables, and low in red meats. Nor did they acknowledge that their industrialized cuisine had paid the price for entering the supermarket mainstream. For, in fact, mass-produced Mexican food shares all the artery-clogging excesses of the industrialized American diet.

The big sales numbers and the mass marketing hide the dual life of Mexican food. Mexicans climb hillsides in fall for purple prickly pears, smuggle seeds, raise goats, snap off a neighbor's avocado leaves, sprout mango seeds in glasses of water, meet in suburban garages to roast New Mexican green chile and gossip about home, gather squash flowers, or pick *verdolagas* just to remember a flavor. This memory-driven market is sustained by regional Latino cultures and kept young by new arrivals, and the second- or third-generation retro-Latinos trying to recover what they've forgotten. It's hard to calculate the size of this "other" market, but a recent study by demographer David Hayes Bautista provides a few clues. He found that more than 1.7 million, or 54 percent, of Los Angeles County's 3.3 million Latinos are recently arrived immigrants, about 315,000 of whom were Central Americans; the rest were Mexicans. This demographic shift, which is occurring in other major cities, drives the Latinization of consumer appetites, as evidenced by tens of thousands of mom and pop *taquerías*, *pupuserías* and *tortillerías*; and the supermarket's Mexican condiment section stocked by distributors such as Roque Olivas, owner of Peru Spices.

Olivas, who started his business in California in 1962 with $4,000, now averages more than $1.5 million in annual sales of 140 spices. The Peruvian immigrant, who packages spices under several labels—*La Preferida*, *Adelita*, among others—says all of his spices sell because recent Latino immigrants still cook from scratch. Recently, McCormick & Company, Inc., one of the nation's biggest spice dealers, opened a pathway to the Latino ingredients market when it bought Mojave Foods Corp., one of the Southwest's oldest Mexican spice companies.

But Olivas doesn't worry about competition from the corporate giants. "California is a big, big pie. They can't eat it all," especially when you have customers who are fussy about quality and who daily add to their wish list of spices and herbs. Olivas's customers are what you'd call *antojados*, a word that suggests both whimsy, craving, and *antojitos*, the dozens of Mexican appetizers from which whole feasts are created. The effort to preserve a culture by reinforcing culinary memory drives the economy of the *antojo* in subtle ways. If anyone should know, it's Joe Sánchez, who, together with his family, owns two supermarkets and the New El Rey Chorizo Company. Together, the Sánchez family's businesses gross more than $25 million a year by satisfying the *antojos* of their Latino customers. "We see more corn husks sales than we ever did; more sales of New Mexico Chile than we ever did," Sanchez said. "On a hot day, ninety-five degrees, we'll sell a dozen packages of corn husks. They won't make the *tamales* today, but wait till it gets cool. They'll start from ground zero, buying the salt, the olives, the pork. If they buy anything canned, they'll buy Mexican salsas. For every three cases of Tabasco, they'll buy thirty cases of Mexican salsas.

"So we are not going to disappear. We'll progress. And the big chain stores will have to stock two sections of Mexican food; the tourist food for the Anglos and the real Mexican food for the Mexicans. And then, since many Anglos like real Mexican food, they'll go over to the Mexican section and buy real ingredients, too."

The purveyors of ethnic Mexican food thus play a position game. Their closeness to immigrant consumers allows them to respond to their appetites. Eventually, supplier and consumer conspire to re-create the culinary landscapes they'd left behind. The *verdurero* who sold my Aunt Estela *verdolagas* brought the border to her street, just as the *paletero* and *pericos* did to mine.

The persistence of Latino immigrant cuisines in the midst of the "salsification" of American cuisine illustrates what Guillermo Gomez-Peña calls "borderization," or the eruptions of alternative Latino cultural habitats within the national ecosystem. Gloria Anzaldúa echoes Gomez-Peña and the "Aleph" of Borges, describing the borderlands as "the one spot on earth which contains all other places within it."

Borderization neither deliberately asserts nor denies a particular form of nationhood. Instead, it expresses a style of being that goes beyond nationality by blurring borders and categories once thought firm and definite. For that reason, borderization undermines the old tropes of national culture by revealing their contradictions. The metaphors of America as a salad bowl have never been sufficiently true. Nor were the nation's geographical, cultural, and racial differences ever completely dissolved in the industrial melting pot and poured out in homogeneous cultural ingots. These metaphors of nationhood presume a society where races and cultures either disappear into sameness or coexist in static interdependence. Consider the salad bowl, a metaphor advocated by the liberal friends of multiculturalism. Notice that the lettuce remains lettuce, tomatoes persist in their tomatoness, in spite of contact with cucumbers and radishes, thus foreclosing the possibility of a dynamic cultural dialogue in which ingredients are transformed through conversation.

Yet, as the nation's culinary dialogue shows, Americans continually engender new *mestizo* offspring. Our most vibrant cultural manifestations, from rock 'n' roll to techno-banda to New Orleans cuisine and jazz, spring from regionally distinct hybrids of African, Native American, Asian, and European cultures, each expressing a unique cultural genealogy. And, with recent studies showing that families in the major cities are becoming increasingly multiracial and multiethnic, the hybridization process will continue. To this extent, then, most *norteamericanos* are, or will become, *mestizos* and border crossers. The real question is whether we will acknowledge our literal and imaginary border crossings. *Mestizo* cultures and cuisines remind us that all cultures drift beyond the boundaries of the familiar. Some are just more honest about it.

But the fears provoked by *mestizo* ways of

becoming are understandable. Almost always, the hybridizing style, because it transcends or ignores the boundaries of the "official" or "traditional" national culture, threatens sacred categories of gender, language, social class, or race. Here in the Southwest, the culture of *mestizaje* expresses a refusal to prefer one language, or one culture, at the *expense* of the other. As a survival strategy, it insists upon violating national or culinary boundaries. These transgressions, however, are not overtly ideological, but pragmatic, strategic, and cultural. The Mexican immigrant who crawls under the fence is trying to come home, or stay alive, not reclaim lost territory. In a game where transnational capital makes the rules, sentimental patriotism becomes an impoverishing luxury. The Latino immigrant's cultural "in-betweenness" is thus transcultural, a style of being deployed between and within the boundaries of the nation-state.

The descendants of previous immigrations may find the Latino border strategy confusing. In one sense, the *mestizo* immigrant's culture resembles those of other diasporas: both try to create a refuge of memory in exile. Eventually, a version of the imagined homeland is re-created within the ethnic enclave. In time, this new homeland is supposed to take primacy over the original, and so effect a naturalizing role reversal called Americanization. For European immigrants who arrived in the previous century, the nearly absolute barrier of an ocean and the limited opportunities for communication facilitated this cultural transformation. But not for some Latinos, and Mexicans in particular, for proximity and ease of communication have allowed them to maintain a linkage with the original homeland. For them naturalization is an option, not an inevitability. Nor are Latinos and Mexicans the world's only postmodern residents. Ease of travel, home videos, and store shelves stocked with basmati rice and dahl now enable the Indian immigrant in London to move back and forth between virtual and actual homelands without too much difficulty. But in this country, at least, the most visible citizens with parallel homelands are the Mexicans and Latino immigrants, a mark that makes them easy targets.

They know the Southwest once was Mexico, and hold to this certainty in the face of border searchlights or exploitive sweatshop owners. The immigrant's dualistic vision reminds me of a Mesoamerican conception. The ancient pre-Hispanic cultures believed the individual possessed two souls—one residing in the body, the other living outside it in the form of a *nahual*, or animal companion. Likewise, Mexicans and other Latinos occupy their cities knowing that each is linked to a nearby double. The Mexican immigrants who cross the border know that Guadalajara is a suburb of Los Angeles, and vice versa; they know that, upon leaving home, they go home again.

Those who believe in the necessity of a national culture would prefer to deny the presence of the companion country in their midst. For some, the idea of ambiguity and paradox persisting within certainty is too much to endure. That's why such fear-driven movements as Proposition 187, the measure California voters passed to deny social services to undocumented immigrants, are so viscerally appealing: They promise to restore the nation to its former imagined wholeness. A moralizing nostalgia, or what Edward Said calls an "embattled patriotism," thus informs the impulse to erect borders around a national ego. But the border-blurring consequences of free trade agreements, capital flight, instantaneous communication, communicable diseases, and the persistence of endemic poverty in clear view of extravagant opulence, underscore the futility of ignoring forces that have set so many people, ideas, and foods in motion.

Still, the neonativists and neonationalists demand that Latinos choose, that they proclaim their loyalty to a flag. Latinos answer, proclaiming a loyalty to their new flag, as well as the ancient landscape that created them (to borrow a phrase from Guillermo Gómez-Peña). Latinos play the roles of cultural cross-dressers. They adapt to their contradictory world as it is, not as some would like it to be. They juggle languages, music and clothing styles, cuisines—anything, in other words, to fashion a more meaningful coherency from fragmented border zones. Sometimes this hunger for coherency can take the form of Estela's *verdolaga* recipe, or the Korean-Mexican *taquería* in L.A.'s garment district, where a bowl of *cocido* is served with corn tortillas and a side of kimch'i.

For the moment, then, Mexican food and its texts express a *mestizo* way of being in the world. When I enjoy Estela's steaming bowl of *verdolagas*, which combines wild weed with domesticated garlic, and Old World swine with New World chile, I also engage an edible text. Her recipe, like a strand of cultural DNA, is also the code by which ingredients are transformed into sensual delights for our spirits and cultural discourse for our intellects.

I would be lying if I could predict when or how the *mestizo* cultural order contained in the recipe will move from our kitchens into the public square or into the election booth. But I do know this *mestizo* culture and cuisine is intrinsically valid now, regardless if it is ever understood or validated by the national culture.

This is not the lesson I expected when I sat down at Estela's table more than a decade ago. But that's the one I've learned. Like messages transmitted from all directions into the center of a spiderweb, I received instruction from a network of female mentors. These women taught me to weave a livable present from their words and memories. The tradition of literacy with which they surrounded me helped me survive with a sense of wholeness and self-worth. For without Catalina, and her female descendants who kept faith with the written word, I would not have acquired either the skills or confidence to write my own ideas. Their gift to me had little to do with the self-sacrificing Virgin Mother image of kitchen-bound servitude steeped in sentimental guilt. Instead, this lineage of recipe writers taught me to trust the life of the intellect, the truthfulness of the senses, and the creative powers of memory.

Capturing the Fire: Roasting Tomatoes, Chiles, and Spices

CATALINA CREATED SAUCES OF INTRIGUING complexity with a handful of Stone Age tools and techniques you'd expect displayed in a museum. So don't be shocked if we ask you to scorch a tomato on the burner of your stove or toast spices and chile seeds in a dry pan. These are the "secrets" of authentic Mexican cuisine. As in Indian and Arab cuisine, the fire roasting and pan toasting of Mexican cooking intensifies the flavors of spices and ingredients, and so gives a sauce its flavor.

TOMATO OVER FIRE

The most commonly used technique for preparing a tomato sauce begins by putting a fully ripe tomato in direct contact with fire. You can get similar results on an electric range by placing the tomato on a dry, heated griddle or heavy-gauge skillet. Roast the tomato about 2 minutes over the fire, turning it every few seconds with some metal tongs. Roasting times will vary depending on the fruit's ripeness. Don't allow the tomato to fall apart on the burners. And don't worry. The burned tomato skins and juices that stick to the burners can be easily removed by scrubbing them with soap and water.

You can also modulate the burned flavor by grinding the tomato with or without its charred skin. We prefer that you grind your tomatoes by hand in a *molcajete*, or Mexican mortar and pestle, because this technique preserves the fruit's pulpy texture so essential to good sauces. But a food processor can work well if operated with a light touch.

You may also need to grind the tomato with roasted garlic, onion, or chile depending on the kind of sauce you're making. Roasting techniques vary. You may stab the onion and unpeeled garlic with a steel skewer and hold it in a gloved hand over the fire, braise it on a heavy griddle, or sauté in a skillet with a few drops of oil. The goal in each case is to bring out their sweet, mellow flavors.

For the next sauce-making step you'll need another high-fire technique to bind the fruit's charred flavors to the sauce. Heat the grease or cooking oil in a skillet. Now quickly pour in the pureed tomato. The puree should sizzle vigorously as it comes in contact with hot oil. The trick is to maintain the sizzle long enough to cook the juices out of the pulp. Cooking times will vary depending on the ripeness of the fruit and the quantity of sauce being made. Preparing a large volume of sauce requires pouring the puree slowly into the oil to sustain the sizzle effect.

CHILES: ROASTING, TOASTING, AND SOAKING

Like tomatoes, fresh and dried chiles often require roasting and toasting to bring out their delicate fruit and nut flavors. The larger fresh chiles can simply be placed directly over the fire, under the broiler, or, if you have an electric range, on a dry griddle or skillet, and roasted till their skins are blistered. Turn the green chiles continually to prevent the fire from burning holes in them. Scorching holes in a green chile will cause it to lose its firmness, which will make peeling and stuffing it a chore. Place the chiles you wish to peel in a plastic bag that can be sealed, or wrap them in a damp dishcloth, and allow them to steam about 20 minutes before peeling them. *Do not touch your eyes. Wash your hands after peeling the chiles.* Spear smaller fresh chiles with a steel skewer if you wish. The skewer provides a convenient handle for turning the chiles—as long as you hold it in your gloved hand.

Dried chiles must also be toasted. Rinsed and towel-dried chiles of all sizes can be toasted on a dry griddle or a heavy-gauge cast-iron skillet preheated over a medium flame with a small amount of oil. The trick in toasting chiles is to use a cooking surface that distributes heat evenly.

Toasting times for the dozen or so dried chiles used in this book vary. It may take as little as 30 seconds or as long as 1 minute to get the desired effect. The larger chiles, such as the *anchos*, must be seeded and deveined. Cut the chiles lengthwise with a pair of scissors and remove the seeds and inner veins, which are the hottest part of the chile. *Remember, wash your hands after destemming, seeding, or deveining dried chiles.* You may need to save the seeds, depending on the recipe. Gently toast the chile skins in a skillet with 1 teaspoon of olive oil per one to two chiles, turning them continually to toast them evenly, but not till they crack or shatter. Blackened chile make a bitter sauce. Instead, merely heat the chile skins until they begin to blister and give off a rich, nutty aroma. Now submerge the toasted chiles skins in a solution of hot water with 1 teaspoon of vinegar. You may need to place a cup or stone over the chiles to fully submerge them. Soak chile skins for at least 2 hours before blending them. Place the soaked chile skins in a blender, add whatever other ingredients the recipe calls for, and some soaking solution. The amount of soaking solution added depends upon the number of chile skins being blended. Blend the chiles skins to a smooth, tomato-paste consistency. Try using as little soaking solution as possible; pouring in too much dilutes the chile's flavor and makes a watery sauce.

Smaller chiles, such as *de árbol* and *pequín*, can be toasted whole and do not need to be seeded. Others, such as the *cascabel*, can be seeded, and then toasted. Be patient. It takes practice to get the best results. And don't worry, you can always eat your mistakes: Dress up your refried beans by studding them with a few blackened *ancho* shards and some crumbled cheese or just nibble on the burned chile like tortilla chips.

TOASTING SPICES AND SEEDS

Seeds and dry spices such as oregano or cumin may require some pan toasting over a low to medium flame. Stir the spices or seeds with a wooden spoon to prevent them from sticking and burning. Use your nose to determine toasting times. The rich aroma wafting up from the pan will tell you when the spices are ready. If the aroma turns bitter, then you've toasted the spices too long. Sesame seeds must be toasted to an even gold color and raw peanuts to a rich tan color. The harder dry chile seeds are best toasted to a cinnamon color with a few drops of oil. The fully toasted chile seeds should crack when crushed with the back of a large spoon.

Shopping for Mexican Ingredients

THE FOLLOWING LIST OF STORES DOES NOT pretend to be comprehensive. That would be impossible since the number of stores that sell Mexican ingredients grows each day. And there are certain regions, such as the Southwest, where Mexican ingredients are readily available. Supermarket chains such as Vons or Boys Markets in California, and Safeway Supermarkets in Arizona and Colorado stock many of the ingredients called for in our recipes.

In Texas, the Fiesta Mart chain offers thirty stores in the Houston area, one in Dallas, and one in Austin which stock Mexican ingredients. The Cedanos Supermarkets has about twenty stores scattered throughout the South Miami area where many supplies too can be purchased. The Jewel and Dominics Supermarkets in the Chicago area also carry a variety of Mexican ingredients.

AKRON
West Point Market
1171 West Market Street
Akron, OH 44313
(301) 864-2151

ALBUQUERQUE
Chile Pepper Emporium
328 San Felipe Road NW
Albuquerque, NM 87194
(505) 242-7538

ATLANTA
Rinconcito Latino
2000A Cheshire Bridge Road
Atlanta, GA 30324
(404) 231-2329

CAMBRIDGE
Le Jardin
248 Huron Avenue
Cambridge, MA 02138
(617) 492-4534

Carduelo's Gourmet Shop
6 Brattle Street
Cambridge, MA 02138
(617) 491-8888

Star Market
625 Mt. Auburn Street
Cambridge, MA 02238
(617) 661-2201

CHICAGO
Armando's Finer Foods
2627-2639 South Kedzie Street
Chicago, IL 60623
(312) 927-6688

La Casa Del Pueblo
1810 Blue Island
Chicago, IL 60608
(978) 421-4640

DALLAS
Pendery's Spices
13350 Dallas Parkway
Dallas, TX 75240
(800) 533-1870

DENVER
Johnnie's Market
2030 Larimer Street
Denver, CO 80205
(303) 297-0155

FORT WORTH
Pendery's Spices
304 East Bel Knap
Fort Worth, TX 76102
(800) 533-1870

HOUSTON
Fiesta Mart, Inc.
1005 Blalock
Houston, TX 77055
(713) 461-9664

LOS ANGELES
La Mascota
2715 Whittier Boulevard
Los Angeles, CA 90023
(213) 263-5513

Central Market
317 South Broadway
Los Angeles, CA 90013
(213) 749-0645

El Mercado
First Avenue and Lorena Street
Los Angeles, CA 90063
(213) 268-3451

Mail Order

Call the following numbers to order products or to find out where their products are sold in your neighborhood.

NEW YORK
La Marqueta
115 Street and Park Avenue
New York, NY 10029
(212) 547-4900

Pecos Valley Spice Co.
186 5th Avenue
New York, NY 10010
(212) 972-7009

OAKLAND
G.B. Ratto & Co., International Grocery
821 Washington Street
Oakland, CA 94607
(510) 832-6503

OMAHA
Jocobo's Grocery
4621 L Street
Omaha, NB 68107
(402) 733-9009

PHOENIX
Mi Rachito Mexican Food Products
601 North 43 Avenue
Phoenix, AZ 85009
(602) 272-3949

SAN FRANCISCO
Casa Lucas Market
2934 24 Street
San Francisco, CA 94110
(415) 334-9747

Mi Rancho Market
3365 20 Street
San Francisco, CA 94110
(415) 647-0580

La Palma Market
2884 24 Street
San Francisco, CA 94110
(415) 647-1500

SAN JOSE
Market Brothers
1670 Las Plumas Avenue, Building C
San Jose, CA 95113
(4085) 272-2700

ST. LOUIS
Tropicana Market
5001 Lindenwood Street
St. Louis, MO 63109
(314) 353-7328

ST. PAUL
Joseph's Market
736 Oakdale Street
St. Paul, MN 55107
(612) 228-9022

SEATTLE
Mexican Grocery
1914 Pake Place
Seattle, WA 98104
(206) 441-1147

TULSA
Petty's Fine Foods
1964 Utica Square
Tulsa, OK 74114
(918) 747-8616

MCLEAN
Safeway International
1330 Chain Bridge Road
McLean, VA 22101
(703) 356-6118

BUENO MEXICAN FOODS
P.O. Box 293
Albuquerque, NM 87103
(505) 243-2722

CACIQUE CHEESE CO.
P.O. Box 91330
City of Industry, CA 91715
(818) 961-3399

Manufacturer and distributor of traditional Mexican and Latin American cheeses. María de Cárdenas, Cacique's advertising manager, recommends that you call her collect to find out where Cacique products are sold nearest you.

FRIEDA'S FINEST, INC.
4465 Corporate Center Dr.
Los Alamitos, CA 90720-2561
(800) 241-1771

Distributes exotic fruits, vegetables, and condiments to grocery chains nationwide; also sells these products on a retail mail order basis.

Weights and Measures Conversion Table

LIQUID CONVERSIONS (MILLILITERS)

U.S.	METRIC
1 teaspoon	5 milliliters
1 tablespoon	15 milliliters
¼ cup	59 milliliters
½ cup	118 milliliters
1 cup	237 milliliters
4 cups	946 milliliters

LIQUID CONVERSIONS IN LITERS

U.S.	METRIC LITERS
½ cup	⅛ liter
¾ cup	2 deciliters
1 cup	¼ liter (2-½ deciltrs.)
1-½ cups	⅜ liter
2 cups	½ liter (1 deciltr.)
2-½ cups	⅝ liter
3 cups	¾ liter (7-½ deciltrs.)
4 cups	1 liter
4 quarts	3.8 liters

WEIGHT CONVERSIONS (GRAMS)

U.S. OUNCES	GRAMS
1	25
2	50
2-½	75
3	85
3-½	100
4	115
4-½	125
5	150
6	170
7	200
8	225
9	250
10	275
11	300
12	350
13	375
14	400
15	425

DRY WEIGHT CONVERSIONS

U.S.	METRIC
1 teaspoon	5 grams
1 tablespoon	15 grams
¼ cup	57 grams
½ cup	114 grams
1 cup	227 grams

WEIGHT CONVERSIONS

POUNDS	GRAMS
1	450–500
1-½	700
1-¾	750
2	1 KILO
3-½	1-½ KILO
4-½	2 KILO

LINEAR MEASURE CONVERSIONS

INCH(ES)	CENTIMETER(S)
¼	½
⅜	1
½	1-¼
1	2-½
1-½	4
2	5
2-½	6-½
3	8
3-½	9
4	10
5	13
6	15
7	18
8	20
9	23

TEMPERATURE CONVERSIONS

FAHRENHEIT	CENTIGRADE	OVEN HEAT
300	150	slow
325	160	slow
350	180	moderate
375	190	moderately hot
400	200	hot
425	220	hot
450	230	very hot
475	245	very hot
500	260	extremely hot

Recipe Index

Subject Index